THE BEST OF
Company

What you need to know,
think about and do to make
your business a success.

by Anne Day,
Kim Duke, Sue Edwards,
Peggy Grall & Anne Peace

Library and Archives Canada Cataloguing in Publication

Day, Anne, 1951-, author
    The best of Company : what you need to know, think about and do
to make your business a success / by Anne Day, Kim Duke, Sue Edwards,
Peggy Grall & Anne Peace.

Issued in print and electronic formats.
ISBN 978-0-9736722-9-9 (paperback).--ISBN 978-1-988462-00-4 (html)

    1. Success in business--Canada. 2. Businesswomen--Canada.
3. Entrepreneurship--Canada. 4. Women executives--Canada.
I. Duke, Kim, 1966-, author II. Edwards, Sue, 1961-, author
III. Grall, Peggy, 1949-, author IV. Peace, Anne, author V. Title.
VI. Company (Oakville, Ont.)

HF5386.D27 2016   650.1082   C2016-905822-0
                                                   C2016-905823-9

Cover image: Shutterstock.com/Africa Studio
Cover design: Megan Barnes

For all content, photographs, etc. that contain specific brand names or brand products, these are copyrighted and/or trade-marked by the respective companies and/or organizations, unless otherwise specified.

For information: www.fullcirclepublishing.ca

First edition
Published and printed in Canada

People, places or incidents mentioned and/or information provided herein reflect the viewpoint of the women (contributors) sharing their stories. These stories are based solely on their perspective. Full Circle Publishing assumes no responsibility for damages, direct or indirect, from publication of content provided by contributors. Views expressed are those of the contributors and any errors, omissions or otherwise are the respective contributor's responsibility.

www.fullcirclepublishing.ca

Introduction

"I read every word of your content-rich and thought-provoking magazine. Thank you for excellent well-thought out articles."

For over four years Company of Women published a small but mighty quarterly magazine called *Company*. It was distributed across Canada and was very popular with its readers.

With the launch of Full Circle Publishing – we decided to revive our magazine but in book format. What you have in your hands is a collection of some of the best articles we published.

The articles have stood the test of time and are still relevant today to women in business.

Our goal is that these thought-provoking articles will get you in the right mindset. Our premise is that success is an inside job, so working on you, your vision and values will enhance your development, both professionally and personally.

For good measure, we've added a bonus section on networking.

My thanks to Kim Duke, Sue Edwards, Peggy Grall and Anne Peace for allowing us to share their wisdom and words again through this book.

Anne Day

Table of Contents

CHAPTER 6 – SALES

CHAPTER 7 – MARKETING

CHAPTER 8 – SOCIAL MEDIA

CHAPTER 9 – BUILDING YOUR TEAM

CHAPTER 10 – LEADERSHIP

CHAPTER 11 – PARTNERSHIPS

CHAPTER 12 – DEALING WITH CHANGE

CHAPTER 1

Relationships

Getting to know you
By Anne Peace

According to the Dalai Lama "The difference between North Americans and Tibetans is that Tibetans like themselves." Do you like yourself? Do you like what you do?

Successful relationships put you in a position of richness, vitality, and success. Let's start at the very beginning – the relationship you have with yourself. The truth of the matter is, as the book says, *Wherever I Go, There I Am*, there really is no escaping from "self" although we sometimes try. Take when we get on the fast lane and don't stop to reflect on who we are and where we are going.

There has been quite a pendulum swing when it comes to thinking about self. When I was a young child in the fifties I learned that to be focused on self was selfish and unattractive.

By the late seventies and eighties, the experts were promoting "high self-esteem," praising children for the most mundane of successes. But constant praise leads to "praise junkies" whose sense of self is based on others' opinions, which can be a very precarious place to live.

This book wants to support your success. For each of you that "success" will look different. Your first step is to have a meeting with yourself. Self-awareness is key to this discussion.

Years ago when I first studied personality and temperament theory, I experienced an unexpected, profound feeling of coming home to myself. I learned that my strength is mentoring, leading people to achieve their potential and become more of who they are. I like me when I am doing that work.

At the Company of Women conferences, successful women entrepreneurs come to share their stories. I've been surprised at how consistently they talk more about failures and struggles than successes. Failure demands of them a confidence and a persistence that supports them living through the failures to move to the next day.

My stereotype of success was much more magical. I thought successful people had something more than me – more smarts, more money, more luck. What I learned was that what they have is more self-confidence, confidence that enables them to sit with their failures and not become discouraged.

This also fits with Jack Canfield's findings in the *Success Principles* that older entrepreneurs have developed a knowledge base, a skill set, and a self-confidence that better enables them to move through the obstacles to success.

Your first and most important relationship is with yourself. Robin Sharma defines his inner success as "a continual conversation and connection with your highest self. Lose that conversation and you lose yourself."

So, how is that conversation going?

Alone with myself
By Anne Peace

Courage is a deeply personal experience. In my work, I witness acts of courage with my clients, who confide in me their deepest fears, deepest hurts and deepest desires. I am awed by their courage to try to put words to their experiences, and to reach down very deep to unearth the truth about themselves.

And as I stay centred in my heart, which is still fluttering, I act with courage. I let myself go to the place that I am most afraid of – being alone.

Now I have the opportunity to face by biggest fear. I live alone, and have been living on my own for the past seven months. I have never lived alone. And strangely enough, here is the truth that I have uncovered. I do not live alone – I live with Anne.

This is an enlightening moment for me. Carl Jung wrote, "Enlightenment is not imagining figures of light but making the darkness conscious. " I have made my darkness conscious. I know that you know how frightening that is.

My heart is still agitated. I believe now the fear is also mixed with excitement. I am freeing myself to live my best life – turning around and staring down a fear that has been ruling my life and supporting me to make decisions that don't work.

I realize that I don't own anyone or anything either. I am just borrowing to help with my own growth. I believe that we are on this earth to learn, and that to just walk into life's classroom is a remarkably courageous act.

Sometimes when I am afraid and I need courage, I wear my father's air force wings. He was a flight lieutenant in the Second World War and flew reconnaissance off the coasts of

Canada. He was a very brave man, and his biggest act of courage was to keep his heart open after he lost his son John at 16 to kidney disease.

My dad used to call me his "little sweetheart." I now call myself that when I need to love myself, to comfort myself, to forgive myself and to find the courage to keep living and to keep loving.

I am learning to let my fear lead me to my courage. I am learning to go inside myself for my answers, to take responsibility for my own happiness, and to live with an open, humble and loving heart.

For me, my deepest courageous act has been to love myself – and to keep my heart open to love others.

Where in the world are you going now?

By Peggy Grall

I'm not really a world traveller in the strictest sense, I'm more of a world camper. That is I've set up house in a bunch of different countries. I added it up once, and it turns out that, on average, I've moved every 16 months since I turned 18. I'm not recommending a nomadic lifestyle, but it has taught me some lessons that I might not have learned had I stayed put in my country of origin.

Although moving is time-consuming, hard work and, if you have any worldly possessions, expensive, making a move has its rewards. I take every new moving opportunity to pitch and toss anything I haven't used since I dropped anchor. Yep, if I didn't wear it, read it, sit on it or, at the very least, stare at it – it's gone! My slightly used life goes off to the Goodwill, friends and family or the dump.

The most significant changes I've made in my life have come on the heels of a good old-fashioned moving purge. The elimination of dead weight, in the form of old clothes, knick-knacks, and outdated artwork, makes a soul feel clean, lighter and ready for the next stage.

And the best part of all this tossing and giving away: a legitimate reason to shop when you land in your new surroundings! When I moved from the U.S. to Europe, I took only the bare essentials: a few clothes and household necessities.

Along with new landscapes, new languages, customs and clothes, moving to another country gives you an expanded world view. When I moved from California to Yellowknife, N.W.T. my ignorance about the Great White North was embarrassing. When you only have the backdrop of your native culture from which to construct your understanding of the world and yourself, it can be limiting.

As we were preparing to leave for Canada, I remember my mother asking me if there were hospitals *up there*. (I was pregnant for this move, so medical care was on her mind.) I honestly had to stop and think… I'm ashamed now to admit it, but I hardly knew anything about Canada. Most of what I knew came from watching TV depictions of the Mounties, and I couldn't remember seeing any hospitals in those pictures.

Having lived in Canada now for nearly 35 years (three provinces, five towns and 11 houses), I've gained a richer cultural, political and personal perspective.

Finally, living in a variety of countries forces you to take risks. Talk about moving out of your comfort zone! Just the act of moving to another country, or vastly different region, catapults you into the unknown in a way that challenges all you hold dear.

When I landed in Germany, I lived with a family who were less than impressed with Americans. They spoke no English and my German was limited, to say the least. By the end of my stay I could hold my own conversationally. And I was more humble and more aware of my tendency to speak from a "we are the best" perspective and, more than that, ready to give that up. I'm not sure that would have happened had I stayed *home*.

So, if you're looking for a "stretch" experience, travel or, better yet, move abroad. And, be ready to be confronted, surprised and delighted by what you see, hear and experience. Travel light. Be prepared to embrace different types of people and their beliefs. Keep an open mind.

Maybe, like me, you'll decide to stay in one country for a while – maybe even take out citizenship. The things I've learned living internationally, about other countries and people have been valuable; the things I've learned about myself along the way – *priceless*!

Friendship
By Anne Peace

"Friends make it clear that whatever happens in the external world, being present to each other is what really matters"

–Henri Nouwen

How true. Let me tell you a story. It's a story of loss, love, and friendship.

I am walking to the mailbox, not really present. My twin sister has recently died, and I am feeling the full impact of the loss of my brother, my father, my mother, and now my twin sister. All gone. They have left me. I am enveloped by an overwhelming awareness of loss and emptiness. The numbness of grief feels impenetrable.

And, there it is, a letter from my mother's girlfriend, Innis. She is 91 years old. She has written expressing her grief over the loss of my sister. She has also sent pictures of herself and Mum at a church reunion when they were in their sixties.

They are hugging each other with joy, and their happy faces reach out to me. I phone her, and she tells me how sad she is for me and shares stories of her lifetime friendship with my mother. The delight in her voice is unmistakeable and then, with joyful recognition, she says, "This is so exciting, I am talking to Bea's daughter!"

Like my mother's friend Innis, my friends are there for me. Food and flowers appeared miraculously on my doorstep. One friend willingly provided nursing care to my dying sister. Another friend offered her mother's brooch to wear at the funeral, symbolizing love and comfort. Empathy flowed like water and quenched the thirst of a breaking heart.

As friends sit in the not-knowing of grief, so too they sit with joy. I often laugh with my friends until I feel as if my stomach is turning inside out and I can't catch my breath. The tears of happiness stream down my cheeks and I leave them there because they feel so damn good.

With my friends, I wear no makeup and dress in my cozy clothes. We eat comfort food together and watch sentimental movies. We are aunties to each other's children. Competition and jealousy are the enemies and, if they exist, the friendship suffers. There is no place for ego.

Long live friendship. I delight that I walk hand-in-hand-in-hand with my friends. This is my advice to my daughter: if you want to be happy for the rest of your life, get yourself some great girlfriends. I did and I thank you all for being in my life.

Getting the issue out front
By Sue Edwards

What's a relationship without an issue?! Relationships within our work teams; relationships with our customers and suppliers; relationships with our managers and of course our relationships in our personal lives all encounter issues.

When we boil it down, we often end up pointing to a "lack of communication" as the source of the problem.

And so the issue gets left there, continuing to fester between people. As a coach, I've had the opportunity to see the results of a seemingly simple, yet powerful exercise that involved placing the problem out in front, instead of between the people in the relationship.

Frankly when I first heard about the exercise it sounded rather silly and far too "scripted" to me, but hey...

First we use a small object as a physical representation of the issue and then literally move it out from between the two people to a table out in front at some distance. The two people with the issue are then asked to move their chairs so that they are sitting side by side. From this more distant and shared perspective on the object, they are encouraged to work together to solve the issue.

Interesting. Think about the last time you had an argument with someone. What did it look like? Were each of you standing on either side of an issue and arguing your respective positions from your perspective? Imagine how things might be different if you instead defined the problem together and then sat side by side to examine the same problem. Isn't it fascinating how often arguments between two people who are firmly entrenched in their respective "opposite" positions end up simply being about two people defining the same issue in different ways.

Recently I had the joy of witnessing two of three company owners wrestling with a very core and sensitive issue between them. They struggled to name the issue and then, boom... the third partner crisply and clearly called it out. He named the thing in the middle of the table, and he was exactly right. The relief in the room created by naming the issue was palpable.

Full problem-resolution didn't come in that first discussion, but the burden was lightened, and since then the three have been able to move to a deeper discussion of ways to address the issue.

Simple, but oh so big!

There's also something that shifts in the dynamics of a conversation when we are side by side instead of across. Think of the times when you've had your best conversations with your boss (particularly if your boss is male). If your memories are like most, you will recall an opportunity for a drive or even a plane ride together.

Think of some of the best conversations you've had with your spouse or even your difficult-to-reach teenager: I'll bet that most of those conversations happened while side by side in a car or on a walk together.

So next time you find yourself wrestling with something ambiguous between you and another person at work – or you are on a team that is struggling with something that is weighing them down, try moving the issue where it can be addressed more objectively; out in front.

CHAPTER 2

Personal Growth

The balance of imbalance
By Sue Edwards

I woke up early to get the kids off to school and prepare for an exciting day ahead. I was debating what to wear to an awards presentation that evening when my daughter called out with alarm that I HAD to see Chewy (our newly adopted kitten).

You see, Chewy was sporting a lovely yellow ribbon. But the ribbon wasn't tied around his neck... he'd apparently ingested it the previous day. I'll leave the rest to your imagination. So an emergency visit to the vet was in order before my already chockablock day. The kids helped get Chewy into his carrying case, and I waved them off to the bus. Local vet sign said: "Closed until 10:30 am." So I drove into the next town to get Chewy looked after. Procedure done, Chewy looked so grateful I had to wipe away a tear.

I got Chewy back home just in time to roar off to a colleague's father's funeral. I sobbed through the eulogy which was a testament to a great man I hadn't known but was able to admire through the words of his son.

Mascara repaired, I set off for the next moving experience of the day.

But first... the outfit I'd chosen in a rush that morning required open-toed shoes. I popped into the nearest drug store for "quick dry" nail polish, then perched on the stairs in the parking lot to do the necessary touch-up.

Next? Off to meet a very special client. His company was up for an award that evening by the International Coach Federation. We had no idea if we had won but my client, Larry, had generously agreed to meet me to prepare for our "acceptance presentation" should we be called upon to deliver it.

It was a wonderful afternoon of Larry sharing with me the many ways that his company had evolved since we have worked together. Needless to say… more moist eyes. To cap off the evening, my client won the award, and my heart fairly burst with pride and the water works began anew.

The various elements of this day, with all of its highs and lows, practicalities and tear-filled moments, encapsulate for me what life balance is *really* all about. It's the integration of a life that's whole, rather than compartmentalized into equally apportioned slices of pie.

I say it's time to throw off the "shoulds" and embrace the gloriousness of being able to dab at our mascara four times in one day and have all parts of our lives touched in profound ways – by family, friends, colleagues, clients, and meaningful work. What might feel like "imbalance" is actually a blessed thing. As the saying goes… "It's all good!"

What are you growing?

By Peggy Grall

Sometimes it feels as if everything is changing. The global economic, political and ecological landscape has morphed into terrain that's hardly recognizable. I grew up in California in the '60s and '70s, when the world was exploding (sometimes literally) with the notion of revolution. We marched and lobbied for change at every turn. "What do we want? Freedom. When do we want it? Now!" Ah, good times.

Well, we got change all right... and we learned something along the way: real change comes with a hefty price tag. Change demands growth. Grow in any area of your life and you will have to change something. The bigger the growth plan, the more you will need to change.

For example, if you commit to growing your capacity for patience, it will require you to change how you see yourself, and your expectations of others. Want to be a more effective parent? You'll have to start by exorcising your own parents from your psyche – and that, my friend, is no small task.

Most of us say we want to grow, but growth demands changes that, likely as not, we haven't been willing to make up until now. And there, as they say, lies the rub. Without significant and often painful changes, there is no growth.

It's spring, and the natural world is waking up. We're surrounded on all sides by fresh green buds and delicate blossoms. All this "newness" has been born out of the dead of winter. The flowers that are shooting out of the ground today had to lie dormant for months. Nature has undertaken a birth, death, rebirth cycle to achieve the new growth now emerging. Without the harsh cold that the winter brings, there would be no flowers in spring. The truth is, that for tulips and humans, if you want something new to grow, something's gotta die.

So, what are you trying to grow in your life? Are you aiming for financial success, greater personal impact, fame or spiritual awareness? OK, then what are you willing to let "die" in you? What are you willing to extinguish to make way for the new?

In my work with individuals and teams chasing stretch goals and lofty ambitions, I've found that there are things they must grieve and let go of, in order to move to the next level.

There are "necessary losses" on the way to new places. Some of the necessary losses are: past successes and failures, limiting beliefs and habits, and self-defeating fears and pride.

Got exciting growth goals? Good for you! Go for them! And remember that early on in the process of personal or professional growth, there will be some letting go, some saying goodbye, some tears to shed, and some stories to put to rest.

Examining your past experiences and belief systems and dealing with unhealthy habits and emotions are the first steps to ushering in a new cycle of growth. It's the way of the natural world, and it's the path to transformation.

Giant Redwood attitude

By Kim Duke

Years ago, I was teaching a seminar (about growth), and a woman threw her hands in the air and said, "Enough already! I'm tired. When can I stop growing?"

If someone had a picture of me at that moment, it would be one of me with my mouth hanging open. I couldn't believe what I had just heard!

My first impulse was to call a funeral home and tell them to bring a hearse. I had one of the living dead on my hands.

However, as much as I wanted to give a smart-assed response, deep down I knew she was afraid, which was creating consequences that were overwhelming and exhausting her, and which were making her even more afraid.

As I wanted her to snap out of it, I told her a story about a tree.

Years before, my boyfriend and I went for a hike in the Muir Woods National Monument. It is a magnificently wondrous and ethereal place, which redwood trees as old and wise as time. I felt as if I'd stepped into a magical forest or at least into a *Lord of the Rings* movie.

The park is unbelievably beautiful and serene. It includes redwoods more than 260 feet high; some are more than 1,200 years old. These are incredibly ancient and massive trees. No matter how old a tree is, be it a redwood in the Muir Woods or a lilac bush in your backyard, it doesn't stop growing. Each year, it puts down new roots and spreads its seeds to the wind and earth.

There is an old redwood tree in the Muir Woods that was cut down in the 1940's – believe me, they don't do that anymore – and it shows the timeline, all 1,200+ years of it. It is a humbling experience to put your finger on the ring that represents the first year of this tree's life.

Think about it. A 1,200 –year-old tree is always breaking new ground. It is always in a continual state of growth.

Guess what? You're a tree too. And so was the woman in my seminar. Even though you may feel as if you can count 1,200 wrinkles on your face sometimes, you're not a 1,200-year-old lady.

Instead of seeing your business or your sales as a chair that can stay the same from year to year, view it as a living thing instead.

Why? If you don't continue to grow and evolve into something better, the weeds and other stronger and more aggressive trees will choke you out. And they won't feel one bit of guilt about it either.

What's the other danger of not growing? You'll eventually "rot" by not staying fresh with new ideas, adopting new technology, new sales and marketing practices. Trust me, your business will suffer.

Remember: not growing isn't an option.

My Sales Diva dare for you: Instead of being afraid of change, afraid of your competition, and afraid of growing, I want you embrace the "Giant Redwood Attitude."

So there.

Looking back may move you forward

By Anne Peace

Growth usually suggests change, moving forward, or something new. Social psychologist Ellen Langer, in her book *Counter Clockwise: Mindful Health and the Power of Possibility*, gives us something new to think about.

In 1979, she devised the "counter clockwise study." Ellen began with the premise that if the mind was in a truly healthy place, the body would be as well. If you follow this thinking, then we could change our physical health just by changing our minds.

She devised a study in which she looked at what psychological effects turning back the clock would have on people's physiological state. She decided to create the world of 1959 and asked subjects to live as though it were 20 years earlier. She wanted to find out, if we put the mind back 20 years, would the body reflect this change?

The participants were men in their late 70s or early 80s, who would spend a week at a country retreat and talk about the past. The participants were divided into two groups of eight – an experimental group and a control group. An old monastery was chosen and retrofitted to replicate the world of 1959.

The experimental group lived there for a week, going about their lives as if the past were the present. Their surroundings, books, food, movies, and political discussions reflected 1959. They were asked to write a brief autobiography as if it were 1959, and send photos of their younger selves so others could see them.

The control group attended the retreat a week later. They were treated the same as the first group, but their discussion and bios were written in the past tense, their photos were of their current selves, and they reminisced about the past but lived mostly in the present.

What happened was remarkable. There was a change of behaviour and attitude in both groups. They were less dependent than when they arrived. Their hearing and memory improved; they gained an average of three pounds; and the strength of their grip improved.

The experimental group showed greater improvement: their arthritis diminished, and they were able to straighten their fingers more. On intelligence tests, 63 percent of the experimental group improved their scores compared with only 44 percent of the control group. There were also improvements in height, weight, gait and posture.

What Langer teaches us is that with only subtle shifts in our thinking, language and expectations, we can begin to change the ingrained behaviours that sap health, optimism and vitality from our lives.

Ask yourself what ways of thinking are holding you back? Reflect on a time when you felt vital, alive and true to yourself. How can you surround yourself with people, places, things that inspire and excite you and bring you to your vital self?

Hey, pull out that younger version of yourself and delight in that person, because what is old can be new again.

Choosing and using the right coach

By Peggy Grall

Choosing a coach is a lot like shopping for shoes, and can be almost as frustrating. You start out with an idea of what you want, pick a few stores, and the hunt begins. It's relatively easy to tell the ones you *don't* want: that becomes apparent as soon as you slip them on. But finding the perfect fit takes a bit of work.

So, with the legions of coaches out there, how do you choose the right one for you? Most coaches offer a 15- to 30-minute complimentary session to help you both decide if it's a good fit. Here are some factors to consider:

Chemistry. Coaching is like dating: there has to be chemistry. Oh, not the breathless variety, but the coach and coachee have to like, respect, value and be energized by each other. Chemistry also speaks to personal style. Some coaches hail from the "kick butt" school of coaching, while others have a more relaxed "Zen" quality about them.

Part of your initial conversation is about getting to know each other's approach and style. Look at the pace of the conversation; do you feel "heard" and does this coach have something to offer you?

Credentials. Not everyone who calls himself or herself a coach is a coach. Coaching has gained popularity as a tool for achieving "stretch goals," both personally and professionally, and the need for coaches to be well trained is taking centre stage.

Find out the training and background of your prospective coach. Ask if the coach is certified through the International

Coaching Federation, and find out what other academic, experience and qualifications the person brings to their coaching.

Clarity. Find out if the coach has coached other clients like you. Ask about their experiences with former clients. You can also ask for references or testimonials, items that a professional coach should happily supply.

Remember, there are important differences between a coach, a counselor and a consultant. At times, you may want the services of any of these professionals, and knowing the type of support you can expect will eliminate confusion and/or disappointment down the road for both of you.

Charges. Of course, no professional engagement is complete until the money question has been settled. Coaches offer their services in all sorts of creative ways; you can hire a coach by the hour or session, the week or month or even by the project.

You could even sign up for "just in time" coaching services; that's when a retainer is paid and you call the coach for brief laser-like mini-sessions.

Contract. Be prepared to sign a contract with your coach, in which you will determine what your goals are; what you want to achieve through the collaboration; and what success will look like for you.

How do you make the best use of their services once you find a coach? Be clear on what you want to achieve and use your time together strategically. Throughout the sessions *you* determine the agenda, and when you've reached a goal, or are satisfied with your progress, you can take a breather.

Having a great coach in your corner is the best insurance for success I can think of, and there are coaches out there with a variety of backgrounds and experiences to help you. If you're in the market for a coach, take your time, ask questions and then give it all you've got!

CHAPTER 3

Me Inc

The itch
By Sue Edwards

After a summer of a more laid back pace and vacation time for dreaming, many of you may be dreading a return to the relative "straight-jacket" that corporate life can assume in the fall.

You may be absolutely itching to get out – to leave the 9 to 5 grind (or is that 8 a.m. to 6 p.m. and beyond?). You long for the freedom of running your own business.

Twelve years ago, I had that itch. I left a fantastic employer on very amicable terms. There was nothing my employer could do to "save me." I was very clear I wanted to run my own show. And there's been no looking back. I'm truly fulfilling my career dreams. But I wouldn't want to mislead… running your own business is not all rosy and it's certainly not for everyone.

If you are debating whether you should go or stay, here are four critical questions to ask yourself.

1. Are you truly itchy to start something or merely itching to get away from something?

Consider your motivation for wanting to start your own business. Are you simply…

- longing to escape a difficult boss?
- fed up with your daily commute?
- bored by your current job?
- frustrated by your co-workers?

Starting your own business may be an enticing escape plan, but what happens once you are out? What are you absolutely itching to do? Could an ideal job, in a better work environment, satisfy these needs more readily than starting a business?

2. Does having your own business appear to be a magic bullet for attaining work-life balance?

When others comment on how I must love the freedom of having my own business, I half-jokingly say, "Yes, I now have the freedom to work at 3:00 a.m." Because yes, I can flex my time to volunteer at my children's school, attend their soccer games and grocery shop when there are no line-ups. It's glorious!

But the cost of this flexibility means spending some nights working into the wee hours to stay profitable. What's more, as a business owner, no one pays you for your sick days, your vacation time or for that matter, your maternity leave. Sobering thoughts.

3. How important is a sense of belonging to you? How will you meet this need?

Many women I've known have fallen out of love with their business because they miss a sense of belonging. Not being part of an organization creates a void that some entrepreneurs simply can't fill.

Others combat this feeling by building a rock-solid support network. I don't mean trading business cards for business development; I'm referring to fostering genuine relationships with other like-minded entrepreneurs who can offer an empathetic ear or point you to helpful resources.

Without sounding too much like an advertorial, this is why many women have joined the Company of Women. They've found a broader place of connection, idea-generation and support.

If you are going to take the start-up plunge, be proactive and do your research. There are many networking groups and associations to explore.

4. Can you let go of the adage, "if you want something done right, do it yourself?"

I don't know about you, but there are no plaques on my wall proclaiming my accreditation as a book-keeper, computer technician, web designer or internet marketing guru. I can't possibly be an expert in everything!

So get help! To sustain your success and your sanity as a business-owner, you must be able to draw on the expertise of others. I encourage the entrepreneurs I know to do whatever it takes... barter your services with other small business owners... invest wisely up-front and establish a plan for the ongoing support that you need.

I've witnessed too many women struggle to sustain their businesses until they've had to "close up shop" simply because they chose the path of valiantly trying to do it all themselves.

So, have a heart-to-heart with your most important champion – YOU! Whatever you choose, I wish you much joy and success in the years to come.

Starting a business is just like motherhood

By Anne Day

I have often compared starting a business with motherhood. You cope with the same range of emotions — excitement about the new venture, quickly coupled with total fear that you may not be up for the task in hand, be it running a business or raising a child.

When you are pregnant, you read all the books available, attend the prenatal classes, and ask for advice from anyone who will listen. Likewise, when you are starting a business, you read the books, sign up for workshops, and get conflicting advice from friends and family.

Bottom line — in either instance, nothing prepares you for the reality.

It is almost as if there is a code of secrecy. No one wants to tell you what it is really like. No one wants to spell out the down times. And no one wants to admit that it was less than perfect for her.

Yet, if we were to be honest, in both cases there are some less than perfect days — well, okay, weeks — when we question our sanity and our ability to manage this new role.

When I was first home with my daughter, I hadn't realized what it would be like to be at home with a baby and no other adults in sight. I feared that a steady dose of this solitude would make me forget how to string a sentence together, let alone complete a thought.

Years later when I started my consulting practice from my home, I felt the same pangs of isolation. This time I had my dogs for company, so the conversation was equally one-sided. And the phone wasn't exactly ringing off the hook at the beginning.

Funnily enough my coping strategy in each instance was the same — to start a "support" group, as I was convinced that other women felt the same way as I did.

When I was a young mom, I helped start the local family resource centre, a life-saving group that provided parents and their children with a safe haven where they could explore, learn, and grow together. Our first program was called *Mothers are People Too* — the title says it all. Thirty-five years later, I am proud to report that this organization is still a vibrant part of the community.

When I found myself alone in my business, I started Company of Women, an organization that supports and connects women in business.

Company of Women hit the road running. I had guaranteed the hotel thirty-five people for our first dinner. One hundred and sixty-five (yes — one, six, five) women signed up for that event. It was then that I knew I was onto something.

Over the years, I've watched hundreds and hundreds of women grow both personally and professionally. I've observed what works and, perhaps more importantly, what doesn't, and I've learned some lessons of my own — some the hard way.

I've discovered that regardless of the type of business, the challenges faced are often similar, and as women we can support and help each other if we are prepared to be honest and drop the mask of perfection.

And in case you ever wonder why you decided to enter the world of entrepreneurship, you should know that, just as with motherhood, there are many moments of great joy and a true sense of accomplishment. Those crucial milestones — when you get your first order, complete a successful project, or pull off a big sale — are exhilarating.

First you sow the seeds

By Anne Day

We weren't at the farm long when my daughters declared that they wanted to start a vegetable garden. Although, in hindsight, it was a bit like the time they wanted to get a rabbit. "Oh yes, Mommy, we will look after it. Oh yes, Mommy, we will clean out the cage." Right. Guess who ended up with the maintenance of the rabbit?

Likewise with the garden, the major watering and weeding seemed to land with me. However, it was an interesting experience and, as I reflect on it, very similar to starting a business.

Being novice gardeners, we started by planting all sorts of vegetables and strawberries. And I have to confess, we rather leapt in and afterwards read up on what we should do — not always a good idea. It was a bit like starting a business without doing some homework on what you need to do and when.

We had a broad selection of vegetables, from tomatoes to broccoli to pumpkins. The first to take off were the radishes, which is when I started to question our choices. You see, none of us like radishes, so why were we growing them?

Watching our garden grow was a lesson in flexibility and not pre-guessing outcomes. Given our lack of knowledge, the weather, and other tests of nature, such as local critters that were also keenly interested in our produce, it paid to diversify.

We planted the seeds too close together, making it impossible for some to grow. And as for the strawberries, they were a complete loss. The weeds grew up so strong around where we planted them that, being true novices, we were unable to discern which were weeds and which were strawberry plants!

The solution? We dug them all up, deciding to start over the next year and be a tad more attentive as to what they looked like. We also decided to be a bit more selective and realistic about what we would plant the following year. We knew more about what worked and what we liked and had a better sense of the work involved.

So what business lessons did we learn? Just like the vegetable garden, when you start a business you tend to offer a broad range of services and products because you are really not sure what will take off or what will prove most popular. But don't choose something you don't like to do, or in our case, like to eat, like the radishes. It's a waste of your time.

You never can tell, especially when you are starting out, what is going to fly. So as you offer a range of products, give it time; you will soon learn what works and you may even be surprised at what ends up being your niche market.

And pace yourself. So often at the start we can take on too much, not realizing how much time all the different tasks will take. Don't spread yourself too thin. Prioritize.

If you have just ended your first year of business, no doubt you will have grown, too, and will be better prepared for the next season in the life of your business. Just like the strawberries, there may have been some non-starters. The trick is to learn and move on.

One of the joys of growing something — be it a business or vegetables — is that you get to enjoy the fruits of your labour.

Opportunity knocks... Are you ready?

By Peggy Grall

To do business in a different way requires a fresh look at who you are and how you exert your leadership influence.

Here are a few ways to wipe the slate clean and turn up the heat on your influence capacity this year:

To be different, we must **think differently.** We must break free of denial, nostalgia, fear and arrogance. We must be acutely conscious of what's changing and continually willing to consider what we need to change to stay relevant, to be leaders. Now's a great time to choose again what's most important for you and your business.

The need to reinvent requires a **new broader perspective.** We must step out of the everyday and spend some time at the thirty-thousand-foot level in order to generate compelling alternatives to outdated methods and strategies.

Business **doesn't happen in a vacuum.** Look around and ask, "Who is living and operating their business in a way that feels relevant and workable to me? Where can I find innovative ideas outside of my industry, and who will go with me into uncharted territory?"

Leading well requires a **clear value system.** As women business owners, we need a philosophy that reaches beyond excellence, past profitability and hangs out in the stratosphere of what's possible! Along with being successful, we need to be significant. We need to turn our attention to who and how we can influence the broader world for good.

Let me ask you: Who's in your circle of influence? And who would you like to draw into that circle? It all begins with a decision. The time is right, the mood is up, and the world waits. Are you ready?

Failure is feedback

By Anne Day

At an Oprah session in Toronto, Tony Robbins questioned why we don't talk about failures. He observed that when people are asked why they fail, the common complaint is lack of resources -- not enough time, money, energy or technology. People blame resources as their excuse for failure. But he said "it's not the lack of resources that cause failure, it's the lack of resourcefulness that causes failure."

Now that is food for thought. How do you become resourceful and resilient? I think much depends on your attitude. Are you a glass half-full or glass half-empty type of person? Is your inclination to give up at the first roadblock on your path? In my work with women entrepreneurs, my sense is that successful entrepreneurs are positive, risk-taking individuals, for whom failure is just not an option. They draw on their creativity to resolve problems and some even thrive when faced with challenges.

In her book *The Secret of Successfully Failing,* Gina Mollicote Long talks about failure as being feedback. You try something and it doesn't work, so hopefully you review the results and take it as an opportunity to learn some valuable lessons and do it differently next time. As Thomas Edison once said, "I have not failed. I've found 10,000 ways that didn't work."

But so often we aren't able to put such a positive spin on our failures, especially at first. We question ourselves as to how we could be so stupid, and almost drown in a sea of our failures. Let's face it: none of us likes making mistakes.

I have to say, once I have gotten over my bruised pride and ego, I do try to step back and ask myself what lesson I was meant to learn from the experience. But it's not straight away. I need to do the brooding, the head-banging and often will hide away hoping people will forget the disaster or error of my ways.

What's that old saying -- that when you fall off a horse, you need to get back on straight away? That makes sense, because with time away, fear can fester in your mind and coming back becomes even harder. No one likes to lose face.

However, while we are all obsessed with what other people think, it's unlikely others are thinking of you, or making negative judgments. Contrary to your opinion, it isn't all about you. People have more than enough of their own stuff to concern themselves with, and sometimes when we reflect back and look at a situation clearly, we will see that this small hiccup is truly not that important in the scheme of things.

That's when it's time to move on. Make your apologies if necessary, note what went wrong so you don't repeat that particular mistake and get on to the next chapter of your life.

Because trust me, there are other mistakes to be made and more challenging situations just around the corner. And like all aspects of life, all we can control is our attitude and how we react.

When we don't view failure as a disaster but as a learning tool, it does become easier to accept the lesson and grow professionally and personally. Keeping your sense of humour is key. Believe it or not, there may be a time when you look back and can laugh at your foibles.

Making decisions? Trust your gut.
By Peggy Grall

Did you have enough information when you got married, took on your current role or became a parent? No? Well, most of life's major decisions are made with insufficient data – but we have to make them anyway.

And the really important choices, like whom you marry, if and when to have kids, and what occupation to pursue, are often made without the benefit of some key information.

The already outrageous pace of business and life has accelerated to unprecedented levels, and it seems that the quicker decisions are made, the quicker they need to be made.

So, how in the world are you supposed to make good decisions when you don't have the time or the information you'd like?

I suggest that you trust your gut.

That's right, intuition is making a comeback. In ancient times, intuition was the "north star" for the reasoned mind. People believed that a "hunch," "a feeling" or a "sixth sense" was their best indicator of which to road to take.

Over time this more natural approach to evaluation gave way to logic, and fact became king in the pursuit of the right choice.

Today, we have come full circle. For most of us, the "facts" of any matter are in constant motion, and we don't have the time, or the ability, to know everything we'd like to know before choosing a direction. And so, another kind of knowing is proving to be a better guide.

Malcolm Gladwell, the author of *Blink: The Power of Thinking Without Thinking*, calls it thin-slicing. Deepak Chopra calls it sensing; my grandfather used to call it his gut feeling; Laura Day, author of *Practical Intuition*, refers to it as instinctual and says it's the birthright of every one of us. I think of it as knowing.

Researchers have recently found that we actually have grey matter – "thinking cells" in our stomachs. That's right. Apparently we actually think with our guts. Or more precisely, our guts think along with our heads. The choices that blend head and heart will feel right, as well as make logical sense.

When you're faced with a decision, whether personal or professional – STOP. Take a breath and ask yourself :

- What is the right thing to do?
- What choice sits the best with me?
- How does this feel?
- What is my body (gut) telling me?

Try it. You might just find that, when navigating a chaotic business or personal environment, your gut may be your best ally. Not to decide is to decide, and it takes courage to make important decisions in the middle of a storm. But make them we must. Next time you're afraid of making the "wrong" decision, check in with yourself at a deeper level and see what you just know.

CHAPTER 4

Money

Claiming your worth
By Sue Edwards

No, this isn't about balance sheets and determining your financial net worth in a literal sense. But it *does* use the "M" word (money!).

In coaching women, I have witnessed much ducking, weaving, and apologizing around issues of money.

This has to stop.

If we are going to contribute our best to our communities, serve our customers as we aspire to serve them, be the mothers we want to be, and enjoy our lives to the fullest, claiming our worth is vital.

Claiming your worth is all about stepping up with the knowledge that the products you produce, the services you provide and the caring that you give have a value that demands respect.

While listening to Cheryl Richardson, renowned coach and author who has been featured on *Oprah*, one segment of her workshop particularly caught my attention.

An aspiring coach wondered how to attract business for her proposed niche, which was to work with "under earners" to help them to break through to a higher level of income. She said, "I've been reading a book about six-figure income earners… but it wasn't so much the six-figure issue that was interesting."

Cheryl stopped the questioner in her tracks. She challenged her with the perspective that it is absolutely *all* about the six figures. If this coach was minimizing the importance of the goal, how could she possibly work with women on stepping into their own value? Cheryl cut to the chase with the comment: "YOU are going to under earn until YOU get okay with making the six figures… let alone your clients."

She explained that we all have a financial set point that our own sense of worthiness won't let us go beyond.

When we increase our sense of value, we allow ourselves to have more. The objective becomes, "How do you get okay with having more?"

In a marketing retreat I was giving with a colleague for senior women leaders, it was fascinating to observe their reactions. Initially almost every woman sighed with longing at the description of the content for a future session.

One group of women said, "Oh, but I can't afford it and, of course, my boss would never support it."

The second group of women said, "This is exactly what I need and I will go get the approval for my participation."

These women were at the same level in their respective organizations, but it was apparent who would be moving onward and upward and who would keep themselves where they were for the foreseeable future.

The reaction of the second group of women typifies women who run businesses that will grow exponentially, who will shatter glass ceilings and who will have the most impact on the world around them.

As women, many of us seem to have concluded that there is something morally wrong with wealth creation, that claiming our worth is somehow ignoble. I would challenge you to consider how you can be both an authentic, caring leader *and* claim your value and grow your wealth.

Thinking that these are discrete choices will keep you small, and does a disservice to important people in your life (including you!).

Are you afraid of "Show me the money, honey?"

By Kim Duke

Years ago, when I worked in television advertising sales, I had a gnarly, chain-smoking boss from San Francisco who said "Kid, always remember, a sale isn't a sale until is PAID for."

This was an important lesson for a young salesperson on 100 percent commission. (Read between the lines "You don't sell anything, Kim, you don't eat."). It was simple: the television company I worked for wouldn't pay me if the client bill hadn't been paid.

I learned to be pretty motivated on collecting from my clients and FAST.

I've sold it – do I really have to collect on it too? One of the biggest stumbling blocks for many women in sales is their fear of collecting the cash. I've coached hundreds of women who had thousands of dollars owing to them but who were still "hoping and praying" the money would miraculously appear in their bank account.

Yikes.

They were afraid that:

- The client would think they were harassing them.
- The client wouldn't do business with them again.
- They had done something wrong and did not deserve the money.
- The client would get angry – loads of drama.

In the meantime, they were freaking out as their cash flow was drying up from all those unpaid receivables. Did I just describe YOU?

Are you afraid of "Show me the money, honey?"

Remember what my old boss said: "It's not a sale until it's paid for."

When you've delivered goods or services to a client and they've accepted them and received the benefits, then guess what? They now have YOUR money. It's no longer their money.

I recently had a client I coached on this very concept. I said, "You don't have to be disrespectful. You show boundaries instead. Advise the client you'll be dropping by tomorrow at 1 p.m. in person to pick up the cheque."

And so she did. With knees knocking she went to her client, who owed her three months' worth of receivables. The secretary told her "I'm sorry, Jim won't be back for an hour."

My client said, "No problem, I'll wait."

And just saying that sentence gave her a surge of power. She realized she was going to wait in their office until she walked out with her payment. No drama, no fuss, no hard feelings, but also no B.S. either.

She waited with a smile as she worked on her laptop. And sure enough, within 30 minutes she walked out with her full payment, an apology from Jim and a whole new mindset that the money was hers. (And she still has Jim as a client, while he has a whole new respect for her.)

She had to ask her client to show her the money.

I think it's time you did it too.

So there.

What's in your wallet?

By Peggy Grall

I'm listening to Dave Ramsey on the radio as I write this. Dave's the Christian "bad boy" of personal financial management. He adopts a "take no prisoners" approach with whiney callers on his daily radio program, and there never seems to be a shortage of people buried in consumer debt and in need of his help.

In her book *9 Steps to Financial Freedom*, the ever-energetic Suze Orman offers a step-by-step plan for getting out of debt. She tells her followers "…you already know why you must get out of debt… Millions of people have done it and so can you." No. 9 on her list for those hamstrung by bills that they can't pay is "You must never let this happen again."

But despite a crowded landscape of voices touting fiscal responsibility, every year Statistics Canada reports that the average debt load of Canadians is more than 90 percent of their annual income.

In other words, Canadians owe about as much as they make in a year. So with all this help available, why are we, as a nation, still so shackled with debt and always seem to be worrying about money?

Because it's not about the money. It's about what we think and feel about ourselves, the world and those around us. At the core of the calamity are our beliefs about life.

One of the most fundamental relationships we have is with our money. How we manage and value our money reflects how we manage and value just about everything in life. Change how you relate to money and you'll change your life.

I remember reading an article many years ago about getting control of personal finances. One of the "money management tips" was to simply keep the money in your purse or wallet in order, that is, to arrange your bills in descending order; twenties, then tens, etc.

The article said that every time you go into your purse and retrieve money to pay for something, you should put the bills you receive back in their proper spot. Keep your money organized.

That simple act of being conscious of where I placed my money changed how I viewed money. I was more aware of what I was spending and what I still had, and interestingly, it made me pause longer before parting with my cash.

This simple practice gave me a new-found sense of power over my finances and my life. To this day, my wallet is a pristine example of well-organized currency.

When I was a single mom/university student, and money was, well, scarce, I used the old "envelope" system. It involved setting up envelopes, allocating my monthly income to expenses (rent, food, gas, etc.) and then putting the allotted cash into separate envelopes, and when they were empty, I was done spending. It was unsophisticated, but it worked.

Do you need to change how you interact with your money? Do you need to get organized, spend less, get out of debt, or maybe loosen the purse strings? Like diets, there is no shortage of programs to help you get control of your financial life. Yes, it's about the money, but it's really not about the money either – as how you handle money is a reflection of how you handle life.

So what's in your wallet?

Can money buy happiness?

By Anne Peace

My father, having lived through the Depression, learned early on that having enough money meant that your family would have food, shelter and health care. When he was older and very financially secure, I remember encouraging him to spend some of his money on "playtime" - more holidays, a dream car – and relaxing about budgets. I still see his eyes reaching out to mine, and with an emotional intensity he said, "Anne I don't think I know any other way." I think he was somewhat mystified by his own behaviour.

He went on to tell me that the pleasure for him around money was in the knowing that he had enough for that rainy day, not in the spending. It brought him esteem to be so responsible in his life - to have earned his money and to have spent it wisely.

He also had a strong desire to provide for his family. He was just as happy to have a home-baked pie sitting on the family dinner table as an expensive dinner out. He was happy about his relationship with money. He lived simply, and no one could have guessed how successful he was.

So it begs the question: What is your relationship to money? Is it healthy? Does it bring you happiness?

When we think about money and happiness, most of us think of all the things that money can buy: the house of our dreams, fun vacations, freedom from worry, and a secure retirement.

We tend to admire rich people and the status that being wealthy can bring. But the truth of the matter is that money is only a part of psychological wealth. Our relationships are also currency to be considered in the equation.

Researchers have found that people who pursue expensive things, material goods and the image they create are not as happy as those who pursue less tangible goals, such as relationships with others.

In one study, American psychologist Tim Kasser found that people experienced more life satisfaction if they had more leisure time. One important lesson confirmed by much of the research is that money means a great deal more than purchasing power. It can mean status, a feeling of control, and enjoyable work. This does bring happiness.

In the book *Happiness: Unlocking the Mysteries of Psychological Wealth*, the authors observe that it is generally good for your happiness to have money, but toxic to your happiness to want money too much. Consider for yourself what is behind your desire for money, and be mindful not to sacrifice too much of your relationship with yourself and others in the pursuit of material wealth.

What do you think? Can money buy happiness?

CHAPTER 5

Networking

An Introvert's Guide

By Sue Edwards

Those who don't know me well often see me as an extrovert. I verbalize a lot and display high energy. They might be surprised that the idea of attending a "networking event" is something I have to steel myself for, even after 30 years in business and corporate life.

While I am passionate about supporting people – the core of my work – as an introvert my primary source of energy is the inner world of ideas. It can be uncomfortable for me to approach a group of new people, and frankly I need to be away from people to recharge.

So, what's the secret to "networking" as an introvert? Here are a few strategies that have helped me "survive and thrive" networking. If staying home with a book sounds more appealing than a night of meeting strangers, some of these ideas may resonate with you.

1. **Reframe your definition of networking.** People often think of networking as an exchange of business cards and meeting others for the purpose of selling services, products or skills. I prefer to think of networking as simply "connecting."

2. **Buy, don't sell.** Instead of focussing on what you are selling, turn your attention to others. When attending a Company of Women event, I often think about something I might need for my business before I go. Then, I make a point of learning about those around me, and seeing whose services might fill this need. When you show your authentic curiosity about others, they typically show reciprocal interest in you.

3. **It's not a numbers game.** Introverts are all about depth of relationships versus quantity. Turn this into an advantage. While others are collecting thousands of friends on Facebook, use your listening strengths to develop deeper relationships. An intimate circle that know and trust you will naturally refer you to others – and expand your reach for you.

4. **Call a friend**. Just like on the game show *Who Wants to be a Millionaire*, calling a friend can be very useful. I often invite a client or colleague who would appreciate the topic at hand to a networking event. Then instead of having to introduce myself, I introduce my companion as a newcomer to the group.

   By all means sit at the same table as your friend, but leave chairs empty between you so that you both meet new people. Bonus: when I introduce a satisfied client who speaks well of me to others at the table, I've essentially brought along my own informal sale force! As a corporate leader, I might invite a peer or someone I'm mentoring who is comfortable speaking to my strengths as I am about theirs.

5. **Manage your energy.** Networking at a two-hour meeting is one thing, it's quite another at a three-day conference. As an introvert, it's important for you to alternate your "meeting people" time with private moments to summarize your notes, go for a walk, or even take a breather in your hotel room.

   I've learned that I don't need to benefit from every single session at a conference. Taking time away from the large group will "restore" your energy, so you can greet others with a genuine, sparkling interest in connecting.

Networking – How's that working for you?

By Anne Peace

I have just sat down at my computer with an empty page. My article on networking is late. It is snowing outside, and I am wondering when the snow-removal company I have hired will arrive. Some days I just feel behind.

I have, however, found a quote I like about networking from Jane Howard "Call it a clan, call it a network, call it a tribe, call it family. Whatever you call it, whoever you are, you need one."

My delay tactics continue and I go to the kitchen to make tea. As I look out my window, I see that my neighbour is shovelling my snow.

And there is networking as Jane Howard describes it. This act of generosity has touched me deeply. I need the help. Then, I remember that when my neighbours were away last summer, I watered their flowers. I helped them and now they are helping me.

Networking for me is relationship building. It is giving and receiving. It is knowing what you are good at and what you love to do – and letting others know what that is.

Sometimes I intentionally arrive late at networking events because I want to avoid what feels uncomfortable. I don't want to be questioned and pressured by someone trying to make a sale or giving me business cards I don't want.

I like the flow to happen naturally. When I am networking, I consider what I am selling and how to share that information in an authentic way. My work is to support the well-being of others and to be an agent of "human flourishing."

I genuinely feel inspired when I tell people how that can happen and how I can help. I am being me, and it is my gift to give. That is when I get the most business.

The first step in networking is knowing what gets you excited, believing in yourself and then going out into the world, where you can best connect to that very personal energy and tell others about it.

Be proud. Be true to you. Be out there.

As author Robert Fulghum advises in his book *All I Really Need to Know I Learned in Kindergarten*, "When you go out into the world, watch out for traffic, hold hands and stick together."

I'll do it my way

By Peggy Grall

Okay, here's my idea of great networking... hmm... I'm drawing a blank. The whole notion of having *nets to work* makes me tired. Most of the networking I've ever done has felt contrived, like blatant self-promotion dressed up to look like a party.

I'm a classic extrovert, but, truth be told, spending a whole evening where the sole objective is to *mix, mingle* and *market* myself pains me.

I confess that I don't actually network much. At conferences I intentionally avoid the between-session chats; I skip the before-dinner mixers; and I slip out right after the last speaker finishes. Don't get me wrong: I like people, I just don't like artificial events designed to persuade me to make small talk and trade business cards for hours.

I concede that my definition of networking is likely old school, lacking finesse and not what the experts would recommend. "Give to get," they tell us, "Don't draw attention to yourself. Be interested in *them* – give something useful as you chat."

This sounds wonderful, altruistic even... but I feel like a fraud doing it. I always feel a bit like a trollop on the prowl, hoping to interest a would-be buyer with a hike of my skirt, revealing just enough to make them want more, but not enough to offend or bore.

But I'm the Change Coach, right? So change I will! I'll start with an attitude adjustment: I'll rethink networking. I'll remind myself that the real goal of purposeful networking is a mutual exchange of value, and that every client, colleague or friend I currently have is someone I likely met at some sort of "network" type event.

I know there's value in spreading the word about my services and learning more about what others can offer me, and I don't want to throw the baby out with the bathwater.

So, this year I'm going to network one person at a time. I'm going to network over lunch, after a movie together or, in the summer months, at a barbecue. I'm going to do my due dilligence and only spend time with people for whom I feel there's the potential for a connection of real value. I'm going to make it personal, intimate and fun!

I'll meet fewer people, but have deeper conversations. I'll spend less time being charming and more time being real. We women have learned that we no longer need to slavishly follow hemlines or hairdos, so I won't be constrained by networking techniques that don't suit. I'll pull a Sinatra and *do it my way*.

Maybe you're like me and need to update your networking repertoire. What will you do differently this year to connect with the people you need in your life? What would networking look like if you did it your way?

(Check the end of book, for the bonus Networking 101)

– CHAPTER 6 –

Sales

Quit cold calling… Connect the dots instead

By Kim Duke

My first day on the job, I opened up the phone book and started calling the people with the biggest ads in the "A" section. I figured if they could afford a big Yellow Pages ad, they might be able to afford the newspaper advertising that I was selling. It was a long day. Torturous. Loads of rejection.

I decided I needed to muster the courage to play "connect the dots" instead. It was the best thing I ever did. Here's how.

- **Look for the hungry crowd who is already buying your service.** Look for people/companies who are going to specific trade shows, belong to associations, sponsoring events, buying advertising, etc. They are hungry. They have a deep, hungry need and a problem they want to fix. That's where YOU come in.

- **Join the club.** Ask current customers who love you which associations, charities and groups they belong to.

- **Ask for referrals**. This is the easiest path and yet people don't do it. You may think you'll come across as pushy. Hint: you won't! Customers who are happy with you will respond to: "Susan I'm growing my business in fill-in-the-blank this year, and I'd like to help other fabulous customers like you." Ask them in the "honeymoon phase" and don't forget long-term customers. Get email introductions – it's faster! *Now ask*! (And then send them a thank you card.)

- **Get on the radar.** Get into the media; pitch a story to local editors; send out a weekly e-zine; post articles on your website that are useful to potential customers; do an event with a strategic alliance partner. Get gutsy.

- **Give out FREE samples.** Make it easy for someone to try what you have to offer.

- **Go for the pilot project.** I never try to convince a customer to give up what they're already doing. I encourage them to use my services as an add-on. Once you're in the door, it is much easier to up-sell.

- **Be the "idea girl."** Be the person who comes up with ideas for prospective customers vs. the salesperson who just wants to sell them something, and you'll see a dramatic leap in your sales revenue.

- **Follow up.** So you got the deal? Send a thank you email and then send a card in the mail. Didn't get the deal? Send a card to thank the company for the opportunity. Simple things count. So do them.

- **Quit trying to find ways to make cold calling work.** It's a really silly way to sell. Instead, have the courage to do something different. I know you can, Gutsy Girl.

The five biggest sales mistakes women make

By Kim Duke

As a sales expert and trainer, I've worked with thousands of fabulously bright and amazing women over the years. Women just like you!

Surprisingly, I hear the same five common sales mistakes over and over from these same women – from businesses of all shapes and sizes.

Unfortunately, you are probably making these mistakes too:

These mistakes are absolute drains on your confidence, opportunities, bank account and money-earning potential.

Are you ready to face the truth about these mistakes that are probably costing you tens of thousand of dollars each year in lost revenues and referrals? Here are the Big Five:

1. Trying to belong to the "Old Boy's Club."
2. Poor self-promotion.
3. Small or non-existent goals.
4. Avoiding conflict.
5. Taking rejection personally.

Hmmm. I could hear your stomach drop.

I would bet you're making one (or maybe all) of the mistakes I mentioned. Yikes! Are you ready to get over hating selling once and for all?

Because really lady – your business can't survive without money or customers. Without them all you have is an expensive hobby.

Imagine for a moment that you…

- Focus on the customers' needs instead of your products and services.
- Realize you have to be in front of your customers at least once per month.
- Dare to create revenue goals that make you stretch.
- Aren't afraid of saying NO to a customer.
- Attract the right customers vs. chase the wrong ones.

You need to quit playing by the old rules. They don't work!

Don't feel that you have to be an aggressive, cold-calling nightmare to be successful in sales. Or that you have to accept all of the businesses that comes your way. You don't!

The most successful salespeople are those who choose a niche target audience to service in an unconventional way.

So I have a Diva Dare for you.

You need to take a good, tough look at all your products and services right now. What is unconventional about you? Why should a customer choose you vs. your competitors? What is outstanding and isn't currently getting enough attention in your marketing and sales materials?

Kick off with momentum instead of mistakes. It will give your confidence and your bottom line the boost you're looking for!

So there!

Still feeding your sales with a teaspoon? It's time to get the garden hose...

By Kim Duke

As a sales expert and speaker, there are times of the year when I'm on the road, away from my business. For most women in business, this would cause them to sweat. They'd worry they would miss out on new business: that money would slip between the cracks.

I don't worry about that stuff.

Recently, I had more than $20,000 in sales booked while I was away – all with the help of automated systems, a fabulous assistant and ... here is the most important part: the fact that I don't feed my sales with a teaspoon. You're thinking...teaspoon? What the heck is she talking about?

Are you filling your bucket one teaspoonful at a time?
Do you remember playing birthday-party games as a kid where you had to fill a cup with water one teaspoon at a time? It took a whole lot of effort and spilled water before the cup was full. I see entrepreneurs and salespeople operating like this every day – running around like chickens with their heads cut off (Okay, I'm a former farm girl) – and believe me it isn't pretty!

These entrepreneurs/salespeople are exhausted, frustrated and have absolutely no time to kick off their shoes and enjoy their business or any other part of their life. How sad is that? Does it sound or feel like I am talking about YOU?

Fill your bucket with a hose!
Listen. Teaspoons are boring. Instead, drag out the garden hose and start getting the hose to be spraying water everywhere.

Instead, you want it set on "soaker" – where consistently, steadily, daily your business is attracting the customers it needs for profitable growth.

Here are three Sales Diva Secrets for "soaking" your business:

1. **Don't let the "tail" wag the dog.** Where are you focusing your time? Who are your biggest clients? Who are the ones who support you, gladly refer you to others and choose your services time and time again? Don't know? Get with it, girl: these are the people who can and will grow your business FAST.

   Don't spend your time taking care of all the high-maintenance clients who have little R.O.I (return on investment). Nine times out of 10, these clients are usually a pain to deal with as well. And they aren't referring you to others or increasing your bottom line. All they increase is your need to buy Tylenol.

   If you focus all your time on the "little clients" (a.k.a. "the tail"), then you aren't focusing on the dog (a.k.a. your business).

2. **Attend only those networking events that are a "fit".** Be honest. Where and how are you spending the bulk of your day? If you are being a "networking nut" and attending every event under the sun, then you need help. Some networking is fine. However, I know people who spend more time at networking events than they do at anything else with their business – and then they don't follow up with anyone!

   But remember that meeting the people who are the right fit beats the heck out of handing out business cards like a poker dealer. Remember: ancient and outdated Jurassic salespeople focus on volume. Instead, you are going to focus on the people who "fit like a Diva glove."

3. **Be in front of your customer each month.** It's simple. Out of sight, baby, and you're out of mind. You bet your customer will buy from a competitor if you aren't in front of them. Or worse: they won't do anything.

I spent 15 years in the national media, where top-of-mind awareness is everything. Top-of-mind awareness means everything to you too. Existing customers and potential customers: do you think your name is the first one they think of when they need a product or service that you can provide?

How can you do this? Seeding with items sent to the top 20 percent of your customers (through the post office) and sending a consistent and helpful e-zine are just a couple of ways. Remember: it is about being relevant, different and noticeable. Otherwise, you're forgotten. All because of teaspoon thinking.

Are you in a Sahara sales desert?
By Kim Duke

One nasty little side to selling is something that most people won't tell you about. It's a place most women in sales don't want to end up…and yet they mysteriously do. What is it? It's when sales dry up so fast your mouth puckers. I call it the "Sahara Sales Desert Dry Spell"!

Sometimes you find yourself caught in a dry spell that will suck every ounce of energy out of you if you don't know what to do. Have you ever experienced it? I certainly did in my early days of selling. I remember it like it was yesterday – how scary is that?

I lost four of my largest television advertising accounts in one year due to changes outside my control. And I was completely unprepared for the Sahara Sales Desert that immediately followed!

Losing those huge clients was a tough lesson, especially as I was a 100 percent-commission salesperson. It forced me to become really creative – and also to make sure it never happened to me again.

So what is the Sahara Sales Desert? You're selling like crazy, working your little buns off and then, wham, the sales start disappearing and you start to panic. How do you avoid the dry spell from hell?

Plan ahead! If you are too busy "working in" your business versus "working on" your business, I guarantee you will have one dry spell after another. You must plan ahead and determine the months of the year that your sales increase/decrease and then create a strategy for what to do!

Have some reserves. (Camels do!) Most people in sales are under-capitalized. You have to have a line of credit and/or access to money to help you weather a dry spell, so you don't react based on short-term thinking and do counterproductive things like cancelling advertising or cutting promotion.

Don't have all your water on one camel! It happened to me; it could happen to you. Who is your biggest client? Now, imagine the client goes out of business, retires or chooses another provider. Where would you be? Don't keep all your major revenue in a handful of clients. Otherwise, if something goes wrong, you'll need a handful of Kleenex!

Make sure you are headed for an oasis and NOT a mirage! Do you have an established sales and marketing plan for the next year or are you just winging it? How much do you want to earn this year? Then write down exactly how you are going to do it.

Listen to my dad (he's bossy too!) My Dad always says, "Dig the well before you are thirsty." This can help you prevent the Sahara Sales Desert from hitting your business.

Now it is up to you. If you are already feeling the heat of the Sahara Desert or if you think you will in the near future, do something about it this week and become your own rainmaker!

The profound show-and-tell experience

By Kim Duke

I love to cook! As a kid growing up on the Canadian Prairies, it seemed a rite of passage to learn how to cook from your mother. By the age of 12, I could make a complete roast beef dinner with mashed potatoes and gravy. Cooking truly is one of the joys of my life!

When I was recently in France, one of my favourite fun things to do was to shop at the local village markets. There's a local market happening almost every day of the week. I stopped at a table where a man was selling knives of every shape and size.

The prices were high, but that's not the most important thing to a cook. What's important? Having sharp knives.Using my limited French skills, I asked, "How sharp are these knives?" The man looked at me and said nothing. And then he provided a Profound Show-and-Tell Experience.

First he picked up a piece of paper, held it in the air and then cut it into thin, clean strips with short strokes as if he were a fencing expert. What was the second profound experience that absolutely blew me away and made my jaw drop? Well, you have to read on!

Are you giving a Profound Show-and-Tell Experience?

Here's a big hint for you. People don't like to buy risky things at risky prices from risky people. So if someone doesn't know or trust you – guess what? They think *you're risky*.

What's one of the fastest ways to reduce risk? Show and tell. (Notice how the word *show* comes before tell?)

Are you consistently...

- **Displaying** before and after pictures?
- **Showing** powerful testimonials with names, locations and pics?
- **Allowing** people to test your product or service?
- **Providing** samples?
- **Using endorsements** of celebrities (if applicable)?
- **Offering** a variety of ways for them to "sample" you (e.g. ezines, articles, printed newsletters, video, audio, podcasts, blogs, Facebook, etc.)?

If you're not? I bet you're struggling. And really – selling doesn't have to be a struggle! What you need to do is evaluate *how* and *what* you can do to offer your customers a Profound Show-and-Tell Experience.

Now, back to France...how did the gentleman give me a Profound Show-and-Tell Experience?

He didn't say a word. Instead, he put his hand in front of me, lifted his thumb, and proceeded to shave thin shavings off the front of his thumbnail with the knife.

He looked at me with a smile, and I looked back with an even bigger one. SOLD! I bought three knives in about three seconds.

I was happy and so was he. And now for your Diva dare: Don't be the risky person with the risky product or service and the risky price. Come up with a Profound Show-and-Tell Experience for your potential customers instead. So there.

CHAPTER 7

Marketing

Creating your personal brand
By Sue Edwards

What three words or phrases do people use most to describe you? In essence, I'm asking about your "personal brand," which is all about the qualities that others *perceive* you as having.

Marketing has a bad rap. Women in particular often equate marketing themselves with showing off. And yet, connecting with others; ensuring your clients understand your capabilities; and contributing your expertise are all elements of marketing yourself.

Connecting with others: Connecting with others is important. You can't be an expert in everything. Knowing a range of people can help you put your finger on answers more readily. And, of course, the more people who know and feel connected to you, the better. Connections need to be both inside and outside your industry. The breadth of your connections brings value back to your company.

Make time for face-to-face connections where you can. The telephone is a good tool too. And don't overlook social media for powerful and efficient ways of connecting with others. LinkedIn is an excellent business tool and it's NOT just for people looking for a new job. Many groups are geared to business owners or people within companies trading ideas with one another.

Depending on the nature of your business, other forms of social media, such as Twitter and Facebook, may also be valuable tools for connection.

Communicating your capabilities: Sometimes people do not see themselves as others view them. The harsh reality is that what others see, hear, and assume about you is frankly all that matters. Perception is reality. It's YOUR job to market yourself in alignment with who you are.

Women in particular are often reluctant to toot their own horns. However, I see it as the mark of a mature and self-aware leader, who can embrace and leverage her strengths, making sure that people know what comes naturally to her.

Contributing: Each time you are in a meeting, you are also in essence marketing yourself. Holding back from contributing undermines how you are perceived.

Social media is an exceptional means of contributing your knowledge, ideas and opinions. These contributions form part of your personal brand, and enhance the value that you bring to others.

Let's shake off those long-held misconceptions about marketing yourself and think in terms of connecting, contributing and communicating your competence in ways that are authentic for you!

The 10 marketing touches you can't do without!

By Kim Duke

I was at a seminar recently and a women business owner was complaining about how slow business was. When I asked her a few questions that dug deeper about what she was doing, I knew immediately I'd hit the nail on the head when she started fumbling and mumbling about "being too busy...not having enough time," etc.

It's like the old song goes, "The leg bone is connected to the knee bone..."

If you're **not consistently marketing:** you're not creating exposure for your product/service.
If you're **not creating exposure:** you're not creating top-of-mind awareness.
If you're **not creating top-of-mind-awareness:** you're not attracting consistent clients. If you're **not attracting consistent clients:** you're not making sales (or enough of them)
If you're **not making sales:** you're not making money.

Everything matters and everything counts in marketing. I said something to the woman at the seminar that I'm now saying to you. Most people don't buy the first time they have contact with you.

It's simple, really. If your customer doesn't regularly hear about you, see you, notice you, they don't buy from you. Here's a scary little statistic. On average it takes anywhere from 9 to 27 "touches" before someone will buy from you. Most salespeople and business owners give up after two touches. Remember: people have lives, budgets that change, new management – there are a myriad of factors that explain why customers delay buying from you.

I can guarantee one thing. If you're "off their radar" for more than one month, they start to forget about you. Here are some strategies that will move you much closer to being noticed versus being forgotten, like last year's runner up Oscar nominees.

Here are MORE than 10 marketing "touches" for you to consider:

- Send out an electronic newsletter twice a month.
- Send out thank-you cards each week.
- Use postcards for special promotions, launches, invites, etc.
- Phone your clients (but only with *new added value*).
- Email (but don't stalk clients – there has to be a reason).
- Join networking associations where your customers hang out.
- Be at tradeshows where your potential customers will visit.
- Have a cool, unique and *useful* website that encourages repeat visits.
- Blog.
- Offer free teleclasses to your database.
- Give free 30-minute presentations.
- Update your Facebook business page regularly.
- Send notes, cards, articles, presents to the top 20 percent of your customers in the mail.
- Write free articles which other people can use.
- Use social media – LinkedIn, Twitter and beyond.
- Use video – small pieces of advice given via video.

Remember: to create momentum, you need **to act.** You need **motion.**

Caring for your customer

By Anne Day

One of the biggest challenges we hear from business owners is finding and retaining customers.

Jack Mitchell, author of *Hug Your Customers*, advocates that you need to adopt a philosophy that puts the customer front and centre. He has trained his staff in his family-owned clothing business to listen to and care about the customer.

He claims that it's good business to become customer-centred, as you give customers what they want, rather than what you want to sell them. And when you have strong relationships with customers, they will buy more from you. They'll also refer other customers and communicate with you, so you learn what they like and don't like, which in turn makes your business more efficient and effective.

In other words, it's all about building positive relationships with your customers.

How do you do that? Here are some tips to get your started:

- Exceed your customers' expectations – it's a mindset. It can be a smile, prompt service, a thank-you note, a birthday card.

- Instead of expending energy looking for new customers, focus on servicing your existing customers better. They can become your best sales force ever.

- Care for the staff. You don't give service in a vacuum. Create an environment that fosters co-operation versus competition.

- Develop a system that tracks your customers, not just an inventory of products This way you know what customers buy and what they need.

- Ask your customers for feedback – you might be surprised at what you learn.

Is your customer just not that into you?

By Kim Duke

It all started with *Sex and The City*. But the line, "He's just not that into you," also applies to the world of relationship-based selling.

Often women entrepreneurs think they have to push a customer into buying from them. And so they begin the barrage of annoying phone calls and emails, all thinly disguised as "persistence."

However, for your potential client this has a nasty undercurrent of "please buy, please buy, please buy, please buy, please buy." Eeek. I don't know about you, but when someone tries to push, coerce, chase me into buying…I run the other way.

What's the worst perfume in the world? Hint: a big honking whiff of Eau de Desperation! Listen. If a customer senses you need the money, need the sale, and that you're feeling desperate – they'll actually question your value. And they will either ignore you completely or they'll give you an outright "no". (And probably buy from your competitor.)

So how do you entice your customers so they are into you? It's all about setting the stage. I know the target customer, and I make sure I hang out where they hang out. How? Here are four tips:

Testimonials. Have credible testimonials from real people, including their full name and picture and where they're from. Talk results and how you solved their problems.

The subtle surround. Find out who knows your potential customer. Ask them to introduce you or to send them a sample of what you offer.

Send something in the mail...but not a big sales pitch or stuff. I've sent newspaper articles or ads I've clipped, tucked in my business card and said, "I saw this and thought of your company."

Get thee to an association meeting. Almost everyone belongs to a professional association of some kind. Do some research. Ask your customers to take you to meetings. Now you're sitting with your customer who is raving about you to others in the industry!

In all customer relationships, developing trust, respect and the likability factor is critical. And the most important thing – don't take it personally. If you do get a "no" from a customer you really wanted, it could be about timing, funding, or they just feel you're not the "best fit."

Send them a thank-you card anyway and stay within the radar. And promise me you'll stay away from that smelly Eau de Desperation.

So there.

CHAPTER 8

Social Media

Social media: Your fabulous unpaid sales force
By Kim Duke

Isn't it weird how sometimes the supposedly "easy" things can be so confusing? Maybe you've been there. Recently I was given a new wine opener by my "evil" stepdaughter. She said with a smile, "See Kim, now you can throw that old hunk of junk out," as she tossed my old opener aside and deftly opened the wine bottle in three seconds or less.

I was impressed.

Fast-forward two weeks, when we had company arriving for dinner.

I whipped out the fancy schmancy new wine opener and proceeded to try to take....the....damn....cork....out....of....the &*%$...bottle! The wrestling match had begun.

Yes, I think my tongue was hanging out while I had the bottle between my knees, desperately trying to open it. You guessed it. I finally said, "Screw it," dug through my junk drawer, found a cheap corkscrew and opened the wine quickly (although I broke my nail!).

I was miffed. I knew I should let go of my nasty old wine opener, but it was harder to change my familiar way of doing things than to learn a new one. Afterward, I laughed to myself as I thought, "This is what my customers are going through with social media!"

Does social media feel like a fancy schmancy wine opener? I think so. You know you should do it. You know you need to do it. But honestly, your half-hearted attempts at social media have probably been painful, to say the least. You don't know what to say or write, and deep down you don't really know why or how social media can increase your sales.

Does the thought of learning some new basic skills on Twitter and Facebook make you want to gag?

Well, I have some fresh perspective for you, cupcake. Here are three important reasons why you need to learn social media:

1. **You create a community.** Yep, there are people out there who are interested in your product/service. They want ideas, resources, recipes, pictures, quotes, stories, advice, tips and more, and you can give it to them. They'll even buy from you. Gasp!

2. **Social media = an unpaid sales force.** It doesn't matter how many people you have as friends, followers, or subscribers, they will pass on your tweets, Facebook postings, etc., to people in their network. For free. You couldn't pay for a sales staff that large!

3. **It's free!** Are you kidding me? You're complaining that it's tough to get business, but you won't learn how to use the biggest free sales tools ever? Shame on you.

If I can learn how to use a fancy schmancy wine opener – and I did, with a little practice – you can learn how to use social media. It's much easier than you think; there is lots of free advice out there to get you started and it's time to get on the bandwagon. You can't delay it any longer.

So grit your teeth, stick out your tongue and dive into learning Facebook or Twitter from someone who is already using it. Do something small. Open up an account. Follow some people whom you like to see, read or hear about. Get an idea of what they do and how you could use those ideas in your social media.

And realize that if you want to be in business, this is a habit you need to learn now. Your future sales are counting on it.

How many friends do you have?
By Peggy Grall

Tena Crow is my BFF, the gal pal I confide in, the one who knows me better than anyone else. We've known each other all our lives, as she happens to be my baby sister as well.

We talk on the phone every week, take long soulful walks, and whenever we can manage it, sneak off for a weekend of shopping or "do lunch." We email each other only to set up face time, and it would feel strange writing on each other's wall. We're "old school" friends and we're there for each other.

But I have a bunch of other "friends" too, hundreds actually. They live out their lives on my Facebook page and in live feed on LinkedIn. I know details of their personal and business lives that, at times, are, well... too much information.

These new e-relationships have changed the way I think about friends and colleagues. Each time I accept an invitation to join someone's network or "friend" someone, I wonder if we will actually connect with each other, beyond my computer screen.

And when someone from my distant past asks to link up, I question whether having been in the same Grade 8 class means we're still friends. Oh, it's kinda fun to see how they look, now that time and life have taken its toll, but beyond vain curiosity, I wonder if we are really friendship material.

Back in the day, a friend was someone with whom you spent more time than all the rest of your acquaintances. They were a select, intimate group of people you hung out with, people to talk to.

Now "friends" are a collection of people, some related and some barely recognized, all reading the same posts and perusing the same pictures. I tend to hear about my friends', colleagues' and even my kids' accomplishments or life milestones along with everyone else, and with the same depth of information. *Is that weird –or what?*

I'm sure all this musing about the state of my connections is showing my age, but it's a change that the whole of society is experiencing. It begs our attention as conventional wisdom about relationships sets aside for a more digital, sanitized human bond.

For business people, social media is shredding the very fabric of traditional TV, radio and print media as a vehicle to spread the word about a company and its products. In the time it takes you to read this sentence, 100+ hours of video will be posted to YouTube. Ignore social marketing at your peril!

As women entrepreneurs we need to select the social-marketing vehicle that best showcases our company, then work it. I concur with Erik Qualman of Digital Marketing for Education First, who says, "We don't have a choice on whether we do social media, the question is how well we do it."

So I partner with Rachel Colic, a young, savvy marketing person, to keep me current. Like an e-watchdog, she nips at my heels when I let my blog falter, keeps barking at me about tweeting, and is gently walking beside me into the new cyber world. Now, she's a new BFF I really need!

Networking online
By Anne Day

In the world of social media, these days you can network around the globe and make wonderful connections through the Internet.

However, just as with in-person networking, it is important to remember that it isn't all about you, and the key is to share useful information as well as promote your own business.

The rule is usually 80 percent information and 20 percent promotion.

Again, it is about building relationships, and I prefer to use social media, like Twitter and LinkedIn, to establish myself as an expert and gain credibility.

Getting started. More and more I am hearing from small business owners that they need to get into social media but have no idea where to start.

With all the options available, it can be overwhelming and time- consuming to grapple with all the information available. A couple of years ago, that was me. I struggled with this form of marketing and questioned the merit of getting involved. Today, I am an active participant in this arena and have tailored my involvement to suit my business goals.

My advice? Get started, but start small.

Choose one medium, be it LinkedIn, Facebook, or Twitter. If you do them all at once, you run the risk of being overwhelmed and spinning your wheels. Pinterest, for example, is somewhat addictive, and while it's fun, unless you have a product to sell, it may not be the best return on your time investment. Go where your people are.

Start where you are most likely to connect with prospective clients and customers. For example, if you are trying to reach professional career women, you are more likely to connect on LinkedIn than on Facebook.

Observe. Watch what others do on the different sites, so you get a sense of what is said and shared.

Share. Provide information and useful articles you've written to build your credibility as an expert. Consider starting a blog.

Circulate other material. Don't write? Not to worry, there is a wealth of information out there. Circulate other people's material. They will be grateful that you've spread their words. Or you could contract someone to write for you.

Find useful material. Research industry online magazines, sign up for paper.li Internet newspapers on topics relevant to your business.

Build your reputation. The more you supply useful information, the more likely you are to be added to and mentioned in online publications.

Consider starting your own Internet newspaper. Using a service like paper.li, you can easily formulate a weekly or daily newspaper. For a nominal monthly fee, you can also personalize and select the content and layout.

Say thank you. If someone takes the trouble to retweet or share your material, thank them.

Follow others. Although you don't have to follow everyone who follows you, you do have to build a fair number of followers, otherwise you will appear self serving and only interested in your own gains.

Be selective. Avoid sending out invitations to someone you know only remotely or think would look good on your list of connections. It has to mean more.

Monitor your time. It can be really easy to spend too much time on social media. Establish a routine and a time limit. That way, you will become more efficient and selective about what you do.

Consider using programs like Hootsuite or Buffer to manage your social media. Through these programs, you can schedule your posts and monitor your activity.

Social media is not just a trend, it is here to stay, and it needs to be one of the tools in your networking toolbox.

In his book *Never Eat Alone*, Keith Ferrazzi says that you need to build your network before you need it. Good advice.

These relationships take time, so you can't call in the favours right from the get go. Become a connector. When you help other people, you get known as someone who helps and mentors others and that's not a bad reputation to have.

CHAPTER 9

Building Your Team

Delegate or die!

By Peggy Grall

You can work only so many hours in a day, and no matter how hard you work, if you don't learn to delegate, your success will be limited.

Sounds harsh? Sorry, but it's a reality that every entrepreneur needs to come to terms with, and the sooner the better.

There is no such thing as single-handed success.

But what's that you say? Can't afford to delegate? Hmmm ... let's look at that. Most entrepreneurs are experts at something. That's why we start a business- we've got talent and our skills are usually pretty specific.

So, let's say you are an interior designer and you, like the rest of us, need to keep accurate financial records. How much of your time will it cost you to do your own bookkeeping? If you're like me, it's hours and hours – because I am not good at it.

And in the time it takes me to send invoices, enter all my expenses and tally up sales, I can meet with three new potential clients and sell some new business. How about you? What are you doing right now that someone else could do faster and better than you?

Delegating to the right person can free you up to do what you do best. So when should you delegate a task and *who you gonna call*? Here are a few quick questions to help you decide:

1. **Is this a task that is critical you do yourself, or can someone else do it?**

   For example, meeting with clients or negotiating final agreements is best done by the owner. Running errands and filing can be done by a savvy high-school student.

2. **How much time will it take to delegate the task vs. doing it yourself?**

   To delegate effectively, you'll need time for explaining what you want, going back and forth, checking on progress, and for rework, if necessary. If the task is simple and you can quickly knock it off, do it. If not, consider delegating it.

3. **How much money will it cost you if you do the task yourself, but don't like the results, and to eventually pay someone to do it for you?**

   I have done this more times than I want to admit with marketing. Nowadays I subcontract my marketing to someone who specializes in it. Duh!

4. **Do you or your network know of someone who does this type of work as their primary business?**

   Just as you specialize in your business, someone is out there does exactly what you need done. Find them, call them, and hand them the work. Then, discuss the timelines and deadlines.

   Agree on checkpoints and the cost, and always, always get a written contract before work begins.

Still not convinced? Try it with a small project. Choose something that you find mundane and get someone else to handle it for you for a month. See how you feel about it then.

Delegating is an entrepreneur's best friend, and if you're looking for reliable people who can help you, ask around. I bet you'll find someone just waiting for your call.

In a great team, everyone leads
By Sue Edwards

We often think of "leadership" in the sense of "managing, directing or making approval decisions."

But think of the times when you've been part of a team and a breakthrough idea came from an individual with a curious twist on how to solve the problem. This fresh perspective can spark as an idea that others then build upon. The willingness to put forward an unusual perspective is an invaluable form of leadership.

How about a time when you've been a member of a group of volunteers that was stalled because no one would step up to take ownership for an undesirable task? Remember the relief created and subsequent flurry of people raising their hands to help when someone did finally offer to take on the task at hand!? Showing a willingness to accept accountability is another form of leadership.

Of course, there are times when "everyone leading" is NOT an appropriate approach. In a crisis where time is of the essence, a top-down one person at the helm is often the best approach. But when the quality of input is paramount and when creative ideas are needed, a diverse team rises to the occasion.

A great team stands out because of how it functions. A great team is one where the whole is so much more than the sum of the parts, and each member not only contributes but plays to their strengths. A wise team leverages what's unique in each individual. In leveraging strengths, each person can provide leadership.

Many of you are leaders of teams because of your business ownership. I encourage you to reflect on times that you've been most powerful as a leader because you've been able to bring out the leadership in others.

New in a supervisory role and eager to enhance their leadership skills, my clients are often surprised when I encourage them to shift their focus from themselves to their team members. We explore such questions as "What would it take for each person in your team to show leadership?" "In what way could your stepping back enable your team to move forward?"

"Recognizing the leadership roles that your team members play in their personal lives and communities, what untapped talents do they have that you are overlooking?"

Ask yourself what would happen if you decided to foster the leadership in everyone within your team? How might this change your perspective? What might you be doing differently? How might you judge your own effectiveness and the success of the team? I wish you well in developing your great teams!

Are you sure that won't work?
By Peggy Grall

Have you ever tried to introduce an idea at work only to have your co-workers say things like, "That won't work here." Or "we tried that in 2004 and it didn't work then – so it isn't going to work now."

Sound familiar? Sure it does. That kind of response is based on what I believe to be a faulty premise. At the heart of this kind of thinking is a belief that goes something like this: if you've already tried something and it didn't work, don't bother trying it again.

Sounds good, but it's simply not true. The fallacy of that reasoning was so clearly demonstrated in the 1978 movie *Same Time, Next Year*. The plot involves Alan Alda and Ellen Burstyn's characters, who meet by chance at a remote, romantic inn during dinner. Although they are both married to other people, they end up spending the night together. They are wildly attracted to each other and agree that, although they are married, they will get together on the same weekend each year after that.

Every new scene in the movie opens with the two arriving at the inn each successive year, always staying in the same room. They never miss a year, and every few years they seem to take on new personas.

One year, Alda's character is a buttoned-up corporate, stiff and angry, while Burstyn's character has just gone back to university (in the '60s) and is radical in both fashion and philosophy. A few years later Burstyn has started a business and has taken on a "take no prisoners" approach to life. That same year Alda confesses to having gone through personal therapy and has morphed into a softer, more open-minded version of his former self.

Each year they have to adjust and reacquaint themselves with the "new" people they've become. They manage to make adjustments, and continue to find enough common ground between them to sustain the relationship for 26 years.

It's fascinating to see these two characters come back to the same hotel room, walk the same beach, eat at the same diner and yet be so very different year after year. It speaks to something fundamental about change, that is: the same place, same activities and even the same intent *do not* equal the same result. Why? Because things change.

Alda and Burstyn's characters changed; they grew their capacity for love, acceptance, awareness, their tolerance levels, perspectives, family configurations, skills, circumstances and motivators changed from year to year. What they wanted out of life, and their clandestine relationship, changed. All those shifts contributed to every weekend being different. Some years it was purely lust; on other weekends there were times of deep emotional sharing. One year Alda even delivered Burstyn's baby. I know – Hollywood.

The principle is this: you or your team or organization may have tried something before, but before is not now. You are different, your customer is different, the market has shifted, skill sets have changed and even the will of the people to succeed may be different.

– CHAPTER 10 –

Leadership

Stop telling. Start asking! Helping others to find their own best swing

By Sue Edwards

Getting the best out of your employees today requires a new set of skills. You need to help your employees achieve their goals, but too much "telling and pointing" will backfire. More than *answers*, today's leaders must offer *questions*. This is the essence of coaching and a skill-set imperative for leading in 2016.

Remember the best golf coaching you've received? You may have received exceptional tips, from the pro, but think about the experience that stands out above the rest. Likely it wasn't the coach who said, "Do it this way!" but the one who helped you find *your own best swing.*

The same goes for leadership coaching. Great leaders know that direction-setting and advice are valuable. But the most powerful tool in a great leader's kit bag is the set of questions that spark an employee's thinking. Coaches help people find their own best answers.

Many leaders put inordinate pressure on themselves to have all the answers. Ego can get in the way. After all, being seen as an "oracle of information" can feel great. While these leaders genuinely want to be helpful to their team, they ironically end up blocking the development of their people.

As a leader, you must relinquish control. Leadership is about allowing others the chance to achieve and flourish. Offering great questions confers power and control to your employees, allowing their egos a chance to shine. So, ask yourself:

- Am I a good listener?

- Do I ask more questions than I give answers?

- Am I patient with employees' issues or do I jump in to solve them before I've heard the whole story?

Let me be clear about the types of questions I'm **not** endorsing:

- Rhetorical questions – often delivered in sarcastic tone; there's no real expectation for the employee to reply.

- Questions to show the leader's own knowledge – demean the employee.

- Interrogating questions – puts the employee in a defensive position.

- Questions to bring you up to speed – valuable for *your* needs, but don't help employees expand their thinking.

Conversely, here are a few questions to open employees up to new possibilities:

- What approaches have worked for you in the past, when you've been stuck?

- What would be a wildly impossible solution if you had no constraints?

- If you stepped back and took a bigger view, what do you see?

- If this relationship were to move from a "four out of 10" to a "10," what would be required of you?

I leave you with a final question: If you were being a true leader coach, what would you be doing differently in your interactions with your team?

Take me to your leader

By Kim Duke

There's a word that frightens the heck out of many women entrepreneurs. And yet this powerful word also attracts customers to you in droves, allows you to charge more and earn more than your competition and quite frankly makes you the queen of your industry. What's the word that freaks so many people out?

Leadership.

I bet you probably started your business because you found something you loved to do and wanted to share it with the world, or you quit your job/were laid off and decided that this was the time to go for it.

It really doesn't matter how you landed in the crazy world of entrepreneurship, but it does also mean something that may not have crossed your mind. Entrepreneurs are leaders, and we have a responsibility to be a leader.

Now of course you should be a leader in your community, your business practices and pricing just to mention a few. (And don't forget about leading the way with staff and customer service either!)

But here's the area that most people forget about. You need to be a leader to your customers. (Gasp!)

The aliens want a leader, and so does everyone else. I love watching old science-fiction movies about aliens landing on Earth. They park their shiny flying saucer, step out of the spacecraft wearing about 50 pounds of tinfoil and say, in a very deep voice, "Take me to your leader."

They don't say, "Take me to the person who can't make a decision."

"Take me to the person who is five years behind everyone else."

"Take me to the person who no one pays any attention to."

"Take me to the person who doesn't have a clue."

The aliens want a leader, and so does everyone else. Your customers want and need YOU to be a leader. They are looking for you to be the leader of what's hot and best in your industry. They want you to be setting the bar. They want the best products and services they can get. They want to buy from the person and/or company that's so innovative and knowledgeable that they are irresistible.

Hopefully I just described you. If you're a leader, I guarantee you have a database/community that is growing daily and referrals come to you easily.

If not…I dare you to take a good hard look at your business and see where you can step up and become a leader to your customers.

Being Vulnerable

By Sue Edwards

People often think of courage as having the strength and bravery to go into battle (conquering kingdoms and slaying dragons along the way). Instead, in my work I see the most courageous clients as being those who set down their shields and display their vulnerability. This is when great work happens!

Think of the times when asking for help may have left you feeling vulnerable or when you may have experienced regret after admitting a weakness or disclosing a need for personal development to others. This is very natural in a society that teaches that vulnerability represents weakness.

Yet, time and again I've seen employees walk over hot coals for leaders who express vulnerability versus those who convey omnipotence. It is difficult to hook in at an emotional level with a leader who wears an armour of perfection.

Much of my coaching work with executives involves supporting them in removing the Teflon layer of self-protection that gets in the way of their ability to lead from a place of true power. They are inevitably seen to be stronger leaders when they are willing to demonstrate vulnerability. This takes true courage!

Leaders who are able to effectively request support are seen as resourceful and strong individuals. When they demonstrate the humility to ask for help, they earn the respect of others. In turn, the leader who asks for help is strengthened by the very support that is provided.

When I start with a new client organization, I have little more than a sketchy agenda and have to work to build a high level of trust between the clients and myself. We are vulnerable with one another, and it requires willingness to work through considerable ambiguity to arrive at clarity. I love nothing more than working with courageous teams that are eager to look below the surface.

Don't get me wrong: it's not all about creating "Kumbaya" moments. A few years ago, one of the companies I've coached was recently named one of Canada's 50 Best Managed Companies. Four years ago, the owners realized that they needed to do things differently and they weren't sure what that would look like.

They tried a non-traditional approach to business planning and did not have a defined path. It paid off in spades. As they now embark on a path of growth and acquisition, they know that vulnerability is a key success factor to pack in their kit bag.

They have learned that negotiating from this stance, rather than one of bravado, is the ticket to forging the most powerful and enduring business relationships.

So, how can you let down your guard and create your best impact?

The Diversity Dance

By Sue Edwards

In facilitating workshops on Valuing Diversity, it's all too common for certain participants to announce, *"It doesn't matter whether people are white, brown, green or purple... I treat them all the same."* They then smugly look around the room as if to say *"Look at how enlightened I am."*

Frankly for me, this seems far too simplistic and we are missing the whole point. For some people, their "green or purpleness" may be absolutely relevant. To look past cultural context, history and personal story is to look past the core of that individual. It can in effect render them invisible. Where's the richness?

Valuing diversity, for me, means identifying what is truly unique in individuals and respecting those differences as their true gifts. In the workplace, these "gifts" may indeed have little to do directly with race, sexual orientation or gender, per se. They may, however, have everything to do with difference in perspective, thinking style, approach, understanding segments of the customer base, being innovative, challenging status quo... the list goes on.

This diversity of perspective is profoundly shaped by our personal experience and cultural upbringing – experiences that are often impacted by what may appear to be little more than superficial, demographic differences of race, gender, etc...

And so, in our efforts to be politically correct and dance around the "superficial" differences, we may miss the opportunity to be genuinely curious and to learn what is truly unique about each of us.

In his book, *The One Thing You Need to Know About Great Managing, Great Leading and Sustained individual Success*, author Marcus Buckingham notes that, "the chief responsibility of a manager is to turn a person's unique talent into performance." He holds that great managers treat each person differently based on understanding each individual's personality, unique talents and motivations.

For me, this management tenet is also one of the most important principles for creating an organizational culture that truly values and draws upon the diversity of its employees.

Studies have shown that, when leveraged, the differences that people from diverse backgrounds bring will enhance the quality of decision-making, increase levels of innovation and create a richer organization.

So, tip-toeing around differences does your organization a disservice. It under utilizes talent. It fosters blandness and mediocrity.

In real life… I have found that making genuine, sustainable progress towards a culture that values diversity does not happen through broad-based awareness programs. Instead, lasting impact is fostered through a willingness for individuals to be curious about one another, to have challenging one-on-one conversations and to share authentic emotions.

Vive la difference!

CHAPTER 11

Partnerships

Are you trying to ride a teeter-totter by yourself?

By Kim Duke

Have you ever watched a little kid in the playground sit on a teeter-totter and then see a bewildered look cross their face because it won't move?

Two potential things happen.

They either sit there looking around forlornly and then finally get off and give up. Or another little kid hops on the other end – now they've created something with momentum!

I've spoken to thousands of women entrepreneurs in conferences around the world, and when I share this story they all nod their heads. Why? Because, honey, they know I am talking about them.

Quit trying to do everything by yourself! It is so great that you can tie your shoelaces by yourself. But this philosophy doesn't apply to business – and especially to sales.

Are you...
- Doing tradeshow by yourself?
- Sending out email promotions only using your database?
- Not sharing costs with a strategic partner for certain promotions?
- Not part of a mastermind group?

If so, you're really restricting how much money you can make. I'd rather have 100 people doing one percent of something for me versus me doing 100 percent alone, because I'm tapping into the power of MORE PEOPLE, MORE CONNECTIONS and MORE OPPORTUNITIES.

Step into strategic partnerships RIGHT NOW!

So let's say you're a chiropractor and you want to grow your business. The first thing you'd do is research all the other alternative therapies out there. Dig into the warm market of like-minded people with businesses in natural healing, meditation, health food stores, yoga studios, acupuncture, pilates, business people who advertise at folk fests, massage therapists. Get the picture?

And then follow my Sales Diva Rules:

1. Choose ONE business that aligns the best with you.
2. Make sure that you like the owner and that you trust the person.
3. Choose a short-term pilot project you can do together.
4. Each partner has to split the costs AND share the info with their database.
5. Both partners have to cross-promote equally.
6. Choose the results you're looking for (e.g., more new clients, higher attendance, increase database, exposure, etc.).

If it works, then RINSE and REPEAT. Think of something else you can do together that is rewarding for both of you. You still have to be working on your business and your own revenues, of course. However, by adding strategic alliances to the mix you'll get that teeter-totter moving a whole lot faster.

So there.

Does your ego or essence drive you?

By Anne Peace

Relationships are what I am all about – and always have been. As a child, I was intuitively mesmerized as I watched the faces of my parents as they interacted, knowing that often what they were saying was not what they were feeling. I agonized over conflict and mixed messages that were unspoken and spoken, and I spent lots of energy trying to make life better. I felt elation when love and co-operation were in the room and expressed by the people around me.

And, as life would have it, I have experienced many partnerships, both professionally and personally, both successful and unsuccessful. I have been a student of partnerships my whole life. Living my life has been my teacher.

So, what can I tell you I have learned?

I believe that it is our ability to make connections that makes us great. It is the absence of meaningful connections that feeds loneliness, depression, and isolation. And I do know that the presence of ego in a relationship can be the death of it.

Barbara Marx Hubbard explains that when you act from ego, you are disconnected, self-centred and dominating. You actually become the problem. Because you believe that you are saving others, that belief diminishes others, and they end up feeling inadequate. She asks us to shift from ego to essence.

Essence is when you are being true to yourself, and it has a ripple effect on the people in your life. You are deeply turned on to and tuned into helping others find their essence. You can go from "depressed to expressed."

When Maslow studied people who were "self-actualized," he observed that they feel joy in the expression of their work. They also find one other person with whom they can co-create. Hubbard calls this "vocational arousal" (and who doesn't want a little of that?). She encourages us to find another person who can appreciate who we are. With that person we can co-create – professionally and personally.

I know that making that shift from ego to essence – some days are better than others – has allowed my higher wisdom to come through. And doing so is supporting my healthy partnerships with myself and with others.

Amazing alliances
By Sue Edwards

Raise your hand if one of the joys of running your own business is having a sense of accountability to yourself and NOT having to "answer" to a boss. I'm counting plenty of hands. Now, raise your hand if being accountable to "just you" is ironically one of the biggest challenges of running your own business. If you still have your hand up, then we have a lot in common.

My business is now over 15 years old, and while I LOVE being a solopreneur, I've learned that this does not have to mean living on an isolated island. I've found that having alliances with other individuals and small businesses provides amazing advantages. Consider whether any of these might apply to you:

- **It fosters accountability.** Through alliances, I leverage my sense of responsibility to others to help me create accountability for actions that support my own business.

- **Offers a natural sales force.** Alliance partners become a source of referral for new business in a genuine and heartfelt way.

- **Fuels energy.** Helping to impact the success of my alliance partners provides motivation and energy for my work.

- **Provides connectivity.** Partnering with others in ongoing relationships gives a sense of community.

Fosters accountability. Does updating your own website keep falling to the bottom of your list of priorities? For many women, doing things for others is a more powerful pull than doing things for ourselves and our own business. So I say, leverage the heck out of your sense of service to others, but do it in a purposeful way.

In the start-up years for my business, I noticed that it was challenging for me to put "write articles for my website" at the top of my to-do list. Responsibilities for others took precedence. Instead, I now develop articles for my alliance partners, which has resulted in content for my own site. A regular column for a recruitment firm evolved into a workbook for my clients.

Offers a natural sales force. Like many independents, much of my business comes from referrals. Because I specialize in coaching leaders who are moving into new roles, it has been valuable for me to have alliances with selected recruitment firms, assessment companies, leadership training firms and software companies who support the hiring process.

For your business, look to teaming up with a non-competitive partner who offers products or services to the same clients, customers, and prospects you want to attract. For me, 30 percent of my ongoing business comes from relationships with specific and enduring alliance partners.

Fuels energy. While I'm a highly results-focused person, I find that my energy grows exponentially when the effect of adding my services to the offering of another business results in success for their business. It's a double-whammy payoff at a powerfully intrinsic level. I relish contributing to the success of my alliance partners.

Provides connectivity. I'm an introvert. On many days, I'm happy to work alone in my office. Yet, there's an important source of inspiration and a sense of support that I get from lunch with an alliance partner who knows me well – or even a check-in call to see how our businesses are doing. It's like having a built-in cheering section.

How might you further enrich the alliance relationships you have for your business and create amazing results?

– CHAPTER 12 –

Dealing with Change

What's holding you back?
By Peggy Grall

I was chatting with the VP of a large health-care organization recently. She shared with me how the CEO position was up for grabs in her organization and she wanted to apply – but didn't. She thought about the position and got excited – and then got scared.

After the first round of CEO candidates had been interviewed, a board member approached her and said he was disappointed to see that her name wasn't on the list of hopefuls because, of all the candidates they had interviewed so far, she was the most qualified. Ouch! She frantically regrouped, but by the time she had mustered up the courage to step out on the dance floor, the party was over. Hmm… tough lesson.

So, what's holding you back from putting up your hand for what you really want? Fear? Fear of *what?* For a lot of people, the obstacle standing between them and their best life is the fear of failure – the fear that they might risk things they can't afford to lose, or look foolish if they fall short of their goal, or, heaven forbid, someone might not *like* them if they changed!

And for lots of women, there's the "I'm not good enough – or smart, capable, educated, attractive, young, old, outgoing, tough, soft, brave, etcetera, etcetera, *enough* – to go after what I *really* want." And so fear fuses our feet to the floor… again.

There's no cure for fear. There are only antidotes. The antidote for fear is action. The best way to push past the fear of doing something new is to *do something new.*

The only real way of keeping fear from stopping you is to feel the fear – and do it anyway. Facing fear breaks the grip of fear. Oh, and the fear of doing something new doesn't get easier with time either, it only gets bigger. Face it today and it will challenge you – wait and face the same fear next year and you'll have a fight on your hands.

Along with facing fear, there is that messy business of "letting go" that must be attended to. There are *necessary losses* that accompany any real change; those historical *beliefs, behaviours* and *benefits* that we have to walk away from in order to move into a new space. It's hard to let go. It often means that we have to leave behind things that we spent oodles of time creating in the first place. To truly transform an area of our lives, we may even need to leave people we've clung to for years.

Here's more sobering news: those losses have to be grieved. Sorry about that, but there's simply no way around it. Start by making a list: what will you have to *give up to move ahead?* Then write letters, cry, throw stuff or create rituals that will allow you to kiss the past goodbye. Then take a deep breath and smile at your future!

Changing something big is work – the most rewarding work you will ever do. Remember, everything's hard till it's easy. Be vigilant in your grief and ruthless in your fear-busting – and resolve today to never have to live with the regret of what might have been.

A stroke of luck
By Anne Peace

Many years ago my friend Howard Rocket suffered a massive stroke. At the time, he was a successful entrepreneur, having founded a well-known chain of dental practices.

He survived and made a stunning recovery. He says he is a changed man now. He wrote his book, *A Stroke of Luck*, because he wanted people to understand that they can overcome any obstacle and come out of it stronger and more complete.

Not many people would put "stroke" and "luck" in the same sentence. We usually don't call losing our job, downsizing, bankruptcy, divorce, loss of health, or the death of a loved one good luck. We call that bad luck. Or is it?

What is this "turning lemons into lemonade" all about? I have to admit there have been times when I wanted to tear into this Pollyanna attitude and attack back with "Who do you think you are kidding?" But my run with bitterness and victimization really didn't take me to the right place either.

In a *Toronto Star* article, Andrea Fitzpatrick wrote about how she lost her Bay Street job and found true happiness. There it is again – turning loss into gain. How do you do that?

For Andrea, it was a little dog called Sophie. She wrote that her relationship with Sophie started to have a profound effect on the way she viewed the world.

And it was Andrea's love of her dog that led her to be noticed by an animal wellness magazine. She now writes passionately about her life with Sophie. "There was not one moment in my entire career when I felt as much joy as I did when I was writing about Sophie. And my growing love of photography was stirring up an enthusiasm I haven't felt in years."

What happened for Andrea was that losing her job actually provided her with the opportunity to find work that was more aligned with her values. She also now defines herself in terms of what she loves, rather than the work she does.

As James Hollis writes, the "test of a psychologically mature person will be found in their capacity to handle what one might call the Triple A's: anxiety, ambiguity and ambivalence.

Anxiety rises in the face of uncertainty, open-endedness. Ambiguity confounds the ego's lust for security, to fix the world in a permanently knowable place. Ambivalence acknowledges the fact that opposites are always present. Nothing is ever fully right or fully wrong.

In other words, can we stay open to the challenges of life and see what lessons there are for us to learn?

As Leonhard Cohen sings, "There is a crack, a crack in everything – that's how the light gets in, that's how the light gets in, that's how the light gets in."

A leap of faith
By Peggy Grall

What would you change about yourself, or your business, if you could? What's the One Thing that – if changed – would change your life?

Take a minute, think about it. Has something come to mind? Good. Now what are you prepared to do about changing your one thing? Most of us have no trouble identifying the things we want to change; it's changing that's the challenge.

For me, there's one thing that needs to change in Canada – the number of women in senior leadership positions. Oh, we've come a long way baby – but there's a long way yet to go.

Where are you on the corporate ladder? Where do you want to be? Women are turning to entrepreneurship in droves. Perhaps it's the backlash to the resistance they face when vying for top positions in large organizations.

Or, maybe they just like working for themselves. Whether you contribute to a corporation's bottom line or to Canada's GNP directly, if you want to raise your profile and profitability, here are some ways to begin.

1. **Own your life.** Whether you are self-employed or punch a time clock, you are in charge of your work/life. Don't wait for the company, your kids or your competitors to drag or push you through this next year... choose your own path. Decide on the training, tools, support, exposure or experiences you need to create the change – then make it happen!

2. **Develop the ability to make decisions.** All of life's major decisions are made with insufficient data. Accept it.

Embrace it. Don't wait for 100 percent clarity before you make up your mind; be willing to choose when you're at 75-80 percent surety. Choosing well most of the time is all you need to be successful.

3. **Be willing to risk.** Not the mind-numbing, white-knuckle variety, but rather the considered, calculated type of risk. Whether the risk is taking on a big project, going back to school or calling on the dream client, take a deep breath and just do it! Admittedly, high risk brings with it the possibility of failure, but it also brings the potential for high reward.

4. **Remember who you are.** Know the difference between your principles and your preferences. Never ever waiver where your principles are concerned. Keep your integrity at all costs; be who you say you are. But, in matters of preference, be as flexible as you can.

So, when will you begin changing your one thing? Is the one thing you want to change in line with your principles, does it fit your career path, is it just risky enough to be exciting and are you 'close' to a decision. If you are – jump!

Turning point. Upheaval. Shift. Growth.

By Anne Peace

More and more I am finding that my early-morning bike ride provides me with an opportunity to clear my mind. I relax and stay connected to the moment I am in and experience insights.

This day my usual route is busy with other bike riders, so I decide, in a moment of spontaneity and confidence, to reverse my route and go in the opposite direction.

I am setting up a shift in my early-morning routine. My route is up and down over hills and through woods, and to reverse my usual path is, all of a sudden, making me even more conscious. Things are getting complicated. I am in a state of upheaval. I am losing my confidence. "Aren't I funny?" I ask myself. I just provided myself with a "transition opportunity," and look what it is doing to me.

As I play out this new plan on my bike, I am faced with many turning points and new experiences. Do I go down this path? Whoops, that wasn't right, I have to go back. Wow, look at that. I have never noticed that, even though I have passed through here many times before.

As my mind frees up even more, I think about myself and all the transitions I have lived through to end in a place of growth. What have those transitions really been about?

They have been about me and my willingness to change my attitude. One attitude I have challenged is my learned helplessness. Take the very stubborn dead bush in my garden that I have been trying to dig out for three days now. As I struggled and pulled, I complained over and over to no one in particular that there was no strong man to help me.

Today I changed my attitude. I decided that I was going to succeed, even if it took me all summer. Then I took a careful look at the root system and figured out where I needed to cut with my oversized pruners. After about five tries, out it came.

But my biggest change of attitude is that I matter. I stay close to my inside conversation and honour and respect all that is going on there. I am learning to stop the finger-wagging judgments and to empathize and support everyone and everything that I'm dealing with. And when I get tired, I lie down.

My terrible perfectionism has changed too. I do my best and let go. That has helped me breathe deeper, sleep sounder and ruminate less.

What's more – and this one makes me laugh – I notice that I don't put the cap on my toothpaste anymore.

Don't worry, be happy!
By Anne Peace

When I was a child, my family would go to the Canadian National Exhibition. There in the Food Building, we would buy multi-coloured candy pills that formed a "doctor's kit." If I was sad, frustrated or worried, I would prescribe myself some pills, take a few, and magically I would feel better.

When I attended the World Congress on Positive Psychology, I learned of a new prescription to make you feel better: a daily dose of positivity.

Neuroscientists are working in their labs and showing us that our brains have a plasticity that we weren't aware of before. This is such good news, because what it teaches us is that we can create new habits of thought that fundamentally rewire our brain.

While it is true that your genes play a part in determining your capacity to feel positive, that is only half the story. We all have choices about how we act and think each day.

Barbara Fredrickson, a renowned psychology researcher, teaches that "Whatever your current circumstances, you've got what it takes to reshape your life for the better."

The active ingredient in this change is "heartfelt positivity." In her research she has found that we need three times as many positives as negatives because our negative emotions are heavier, and human nature is to turn toward the downward spiral. She is teaching us to create an upward spiral.

As a child, I was full of optimism and hope, but it was my "pills" that brought me to an upward spiral. Obviously they were a placebo, but does that matter? They gave me independence – a sense that I could control my emotions and how I felt about the world.

As adults we have choices. We can make the choice to emphasize the positive emotions of joy, love, hope, interest, awe, inspiration, amusement, pride, serenity and hope. We can show our children that they have choices too.

This state of mind can enhance your relationships, improve your health, relieve depression and broaden your mind. This is one bandwagon I believe in, and I'm happy to climb onboard.

– BONUS –

Networking 101

By
Anne Day

*"The currency of real networking is not greed,
but generosity"*

– Keith Ferrazzi

Just as location, location, location is vital in real estate, networking, networking, networking is crucial to your business growth.

Yet networking gets a bad rap.

It conjures up images of a used-car salesman with slicked back hair trying to persuade you that the car in front of you has your name on it. Yuck.

Several people now use the word "net-weaving," and I much prefer this vocabulary.

In fact, when I started Company of Women, I used tapestries on my business cards, website, and banner. I felt they symbolized intertwined threads, creating a strong, beautiful fabric.

Part of the problem with networking is that no one teaches you how to do it.

Sadly, there are still folks out there who believe it is about collecting as many business cards as possible at a networking event, because it is all about them.

That's what I call the "business card shuffle," and it's a game I don't encourage you to play.

It is often said that people do business with people they know and trust. That takes time. It's about building relationships, and that's not something you can do just by thrusting your business card in someone's hand and moving on to pounce on your next prey.

I recently read a great analogy that described the card collector as a hunter and the person taking time to get to know you as a farmer. The hunter was predatory; the farmer nurtured the relationship.

Which are you?

When I first had my consulting practice, I joined a networking group. At that time, I was often hired by the government to work with non- profits, so getting business from the other participants really wasn't my goal. No. I wanted to connect with other business women as I found it lonely working at home and wanted to meet up with other professional women.

What I found at these events was that most people would ask what I did, and after I said I worked in social services, their eyes would glaze over. I could sense those people looking over my shoulder to see who they wanted to meet next. Then they would quickly hand me a card and move on.

To me there is nothing meaningful in that kind of interaction, and it was one of the reasons I started Company of Women.

Getting started

Before attending any event, do your homework. There are so many networks out there that you could eat your way through each day—breakfast, lunch, and dinner—to build your business.

Ask around. Find out which networks are worth attending. I usually encourage women to be part of three networks (if they can afford it):

1. The local chamber, as this gives you credibility
2. A women-only network, as we do business differently and are supportive of each other.

3. An industry-related network, where you can keep informed and connected with your peers and find opportunities to partner together on projects.

Remember, not all networks are created equal. Some are mainly social and help reduce the isolation you can feel, especially if you have just started out.

Some are very specific, like mompreneurs, who want to connect with other women who are juggling their business ventures with raising a family.

Others are more regulated. They only accept one person per category/industry; you meet weekly and are expected to give referrals within the group. Then there are networks like Company of Women, where the focus is on education and learning the tools of business while supporting and connecting with one another.

Shop around. Most networks will let you come as a guest. See what is a fit for you. Also, spend some time thinking about what you want to get out of a network. If getting business is your main goal, then you need to connect with your potential clients. Think about where they go and how you can meet them.

But don't forget that even if the person you meet at a networking event doesn't end up becoming your customer, she may well introduce you to someone who does.

When are you at your best? Think about your lifestyle. Are you a morning person or a night owl? What works for your family? If you have children to get off to school, the 7.30 a.m. breakfast meeting may not suit you.

Business cards. Don't leave home without them! While I don't encourage playing the business card shuffle, you do need business cards. They should include your contact information and if there's room, how to connect with you on social media. They don't have to be fancy, and places like Vista Print can produce them quite quickly and cheaply.

And have your cards on you at all times, because you never know who you are going to bump into socially, and having a card handy helps to make the connection.

Ready, set, go... You've decided to go and check out one of two events. If you're a real introvert, take a buddy with you. It's far easier to walk into a room of strangers with a friend by your side. Here are some other pointers:

- Have some goals in mind. Before you set out, think what you'd like to achieve, but keep those goals realistic. It is highly unlikely that you will leave that first meeting with business in hand.

- Personally, rather than "work the room," I would spend my time with one or two people, have a meaningful discussion, and get to know about their businesses.

- Often when I go to an event where I don't know anyone, I look for a friendly face or someone who, like me, doesn't seem to know anyone, and I start a conversation.

- If two or more people are deep in conversation, that is not the group to try and join. Watch for the body language. You don't want to interrupt.

- Act the part. Start with a hello and a smile. When you smile at someone and they smile back, it leads the way to friendly communication.

- Give a firm handshake. Be proactive. Be the first to extend your hand. Develop a firm and confident handshake.

- Make and keep eye contact. Eye contact is the first step to making a strong connection with another person.

- Stay focused. Concentrate on the person you are talking to and listen attentively.

- Keep one pocket for your cards and another for the cards you receive. You want to be sure it's your card you're giving out!

- If you are given a name tag, wear it on your right side so that when people shake your hand, they can see your name.

- It's not all about you. Take an interest. Rather than launching in to what you do, ask about the other person. Have some open-ended questions in your back pocket.

Conversation starters

- Is this your first meeting with this group?

- What brought you along tonight/this morning?

- Have you heard the speaker before?

- What business are you in?

- Who would be your ideal customer?

- How long have you been in business?

- And if all else fails, talk about the weather!

Think about who you know that you can connect the person with—a potential customer, an alliance. Even if you can't use the person's service or are not interested in their product, chances are you may know someone who is. When you help someone, they are more likely to help you.

You never know who knows who. It truly is six degrees of separation. And you just never know when you are going to meet someone who has the right connections for you.

It could be at a social event, at the hairdressers, whatever. Have your business cards with you, and when you change purses, move your cards too.

Tell stories. When someone does ask what you do, have some stories to tell that illustrate your work and how you help people.

Avoid jargon or no one will understand you. And stay away from the slick infomercial. To me, it just comes across as insincere and rehearsed.

Learn how to extricate yourself
One of the challenges of networking is when you get stuck with one person, and it is time for you to move on.

Here are a few ways you can extricate yourself diplomatically:

- Find someone else to introduce the person to. Take them over, and then leave.

- Say you've just spotted someone you need to speak to.

- Thank them for the conversation and say that you don't want to take up any more of their time.

- If all else fails, have a washroom break, get some food, whatever...

Follow up

Making all these connections is for naught if you don't do the follow up. If you have said you will do something, do it. Send the article, make the introduction. I usually write the commitment on the back of the business card so I don't forget.

With the new anti-spam laws, remember you can't just add people to your mailing list without permission. So ask. I have found that sending articles is one way to stay in touch, and it earns you brownie points with the recipient.

Set up one-on-one meetings for coffee to discuss further how you can help each other, but be respectful of people's time. Avoid saying that you want to "pick someone's brain" about something. For me, that's a red flag that someone wants to take up my time and get my expertise for free.

Got a satisfied customer? Ask for a referral. Word of mouth promotion is the best marketing you can get and it's free.

Conferences

If you are going with friends, split up. If you are there to network, you are less likely to do it if you are sitting with your friends all the time. At our conference, we actually pre-assign people to different tables throughout the day. So you could say we force people to mix and mingle.

But the truth is, you are not going to meet new folks and drum up new business if you stay with your friends. I personally find conferences great for recruiting new members. Whoever has the (mis)fortune to sit next to me ends up joining Company of Women!

Trade shows

Having a booth at a trade show is something to be considered seriously.

Often, they are expensive so you need to do your math ahead of time and determine how many widgets, for example, you have to sell for it to be worthwhile.

Now, making sales is not the only reason to do a trade show, often it is as much about creating awareness.

Also, do your homework about the actual show and ask questions:

- How long has the organization been doing this event?

- How many people will be attending?

- What is the demographic?

- Are there additional costs?

I suggest these questions, because I learned the answers the hard way. The first trade show we ever participated in, I went all out, hired people to help me for the two-day event, got banners, and had 3,000 give-away buttons made, as I was told this was the number to expect.

What I neglected to find out was whether this was the first time the organizers had delivered the show. And while their goal may have been 3,000, in reality it was 500. And today I still have those buttons as a reminder of what I neglected to find out!

At another show, we met with similar results. This time I discovered that most of the participants were male and that we had to pay extra for electrical, tables, chairs, etc. What started as a reasonable price quickly snowballed into something way more expensive, and although the participants were small business owners, they were the wrong gender for our business.

Having an attractive booth, with some interactive activity, will draw people in. You do need a give-away item and a way to collect business cards so you can follow up later. But remember the anti-spam laws.

You also need to train your team, so they look engaged, are interesting, and can talk comfortably about your product and service. What you don't want is someone sitting behind the booth table, reading or, worse still, knitting. Definitely gives the wrong impression!

Talking about sitting, trade shows are hard on your legs and feet. Bring a change of shoes, and have shifts so members of your team can take a break and sit   down.

Measure the results, so you know whether it is worth your time and money to   participate again next year.

And remember as Darcy Rezac says "You have to kiss a lot of frogs before you get a prince."

Meet the Authors

Anne Day

Award-winning entrepreneur Anne Day is the founder of Company of Women, an organization she started in 2003 to support, connect and promote women in business through its events, annual conference, online publications, and extensive website.

Over the years, Anne has worked with thousands of women entrepreneurs, and as an entrepreneur herself, is fully aware of the trials and triumphs of building and growing a business.

She is the author/editor of four books on women and entrepreneurship and a regular columnist with the Huffington Post as well as other online publications. She is the President of Full Circle Publishing, working with writers to get their words out into the world.

Anne has had an eclectic career from leadership roles in the non-profit sector, editor of a national magazine to working in government on women's issues. She has received numerous awards for her work, which has always focused on the needs of women. She is married with two daughters and lives on a farm in Ontario, Canada.

Websites www.companyofwomen.ca and www.fullcirclepublishing.ca

You can reach Anne at anne@fullcirclepublishing.ca or anneday@companyofwomen.ca

Kim Duke

Kim Duke is Founder of salesdivas.com, she's an international sales speaker, coach and Amazon best-selling author who provides savvy, sassy sales training for women entrepreneurs and sales people.

Her extensive sales background was based in the media – 15 years working with two of Canada's largest national television networks in sales and management.

Now Kim is a successful 14 year entrepreneur – providing sales training for companies and conferences internationally. (She recently spoke in London, England!) She has presented for organizations such as the US Small Business Administration, the NBA (National Basketball Association), major Canadian and American franchises, direct sales organizations as well as business conferences around the world.

She's an Amazon Best-Selling author of *Ugly Baby: How To Get Over Fear and Give Birth To Your Odd Idea, Start A Business or Invent Something Cool.*

She's had numerous interviews for international television, radio and print (She was featured on NBC Television and was in the March 2014 issue of Cosmopolitan Magazine) Kim has over 30,000 women entrepreneurs from 54 countries around the world who eagerly await her sales tips each week.

www.salesdivas.com

Sue Edwards

Sue Edwards is an Executive Coach who works with business owners and organization leaders.

She has received the prestigious PRISM Award from the International Coach Federation-GTA Chapter for her work with a mid-sized infrastructure & road building company, recognizing enhanced business performance through commitment to coaching as a leadership strategy. This company was also named as one of Canada's 50 Best Managed Companies.

Sue's clients value her integrity, pragmatism, and willingness to challenge. "Saying what needs to be said" is core to the successful track record of her coaching relationships. She is adept at supporting leaders in establishing their authentic strength by accessing their vulnerability.

Sue has written numerous articles on leadership and entrepreneurship. She has authored a self-coaching workbook called, *Wow Them In Your New Job! (and reduce your overwhelm)...It's Easier Than You'd Expect.* She is a contributing author to *Awakening the Workplace 2* and *Leadership Gurus Speak Out.*

Sue is certified in the use of various assessment instruments, including MBTI, DISC, Profile XT and Benchmarks® 360. She is a frequent speaker at international conferences.

Sue founded her management consulting and coaching firm in 1996. She has extensive business experience in senior human resources positions with Imperial Oil, Bayer and Campbell Soup. She is a proud Mom of two teens and two cats and is an adept chauffeur.

Susan P. Edwards, PCC, CHRP
President, Development by Design
http://www.constructionleadershipcoach.com

Peggy Grall

Peggy Grall brings the love of people and change to her work. The *Toronto Star* calls Peggy, 'Tonic for the transition challenged' and her clients know she's the change agent you want in your corner when the going gets tough.

She is a Certified Business Coach and former Psychotherapist with 23 years experience transitioning people through organizational change and crisis. Peggy works closely with senior leadership teams that are experiencing increasingly complex change, helping them to anticipate, plan for and execute CM best practices. As well, she trains leaders and managers in the art of *coaching for engagement.*

Peggy is an internationally recognized keynote speaker and author of *Just Change It!* As well as the popular training game *Transition Poker™.* She's the Toronto Chapter Chair for three chapters of the Women President's Organization, a non-profit organization that gathers female owners of multi-million dollar companies to share and learn from each other.

Peggy also coaches and trains international Non-Profit leaders through the Arrow Leadership Program. Peggy has worked with Staples, Magna, Johnson & Jonson, Scotia Bank, several health care organizations and many of the universities across Ontario.

www.peggygrall.com

Anne sees life as an adventure, an adventure that she fully engages in, bringing joy and vitality to herself and to others.

She knows that we can all creatively express ourselves to live the life that we can feel passionate about and that honours our unique abilities and needs.

Anne Peace

As a public health nurse, early childhood educator and personal life coach she has chosen careers where she can be in authentic partnership with those clients and students she is supporting and is in conversation with. She sees herself as an agent of human flourishing.

As an author she believes in telling the story of her own life and sharing the wisdom that she has learned.

She feels gratitude for the simple joys of life and takes time to express her thanks.

She feels JOY often and makes choices daily to bring more joy in to her life and the lives of others.

And she giggles as she now calls herself a JOYOLOGIST.